"I'm always impressed by people who live life as an adventure yet remain unashamedly human in the telling of the tale. Nathan Schnackenberg's story will take you round the world from Japan to Las Vegas to Afghanistan. In years gone by we would have gathered eagerly round fires to hear such tales of risk and redemption. This book is the next best thing. Read it!"
—*PETE GREIG*, founder, 24-7 Prayer

WHEN THE ROAD TO REBELLION LEADS YOU STRAIGHT TO GOD

Nathan Schnackenberg

PATHWAYS TO ABANDON

[RELEVANTBOOKS]

Published by Relevant Books
A division of Relevant Media Group, Inc.

www.relevantbooks.com
www.relevantmediagroup.com

© 2005 Relevant Media Group

Cover design by Mark Arnold
Interior design by Jeremy Kennedy, Aaron Maurer
Contributing photography by Mary Tamaki, Makkai Bence

Library of Congress Control Number: 2005902184
International Standard Book Number: 0976364220

For information or bulk orders:
RELEVANT MEDIA GROUP, INC.
100 SOUTH LAKE DESTINY DR. STE. 200
ORLANDO, FL 32810
407-660-1411

05 06 07 08 9 8 7 6 5 4 3 2 1

Printed in the United States of America

CONTENTS

INTRODUCTION
A CONFIRMATION

By Jeremy Barnett:

I moved to Colorado because I was suffering from a crack addiction. I knew that living near my parents could help me recover from the ups and downs of post-addiction. After working various jobs, an elder from my church hired me to work in his travel agency. From the get-go, I was transparent with my colleagues, all who were believers, and at the time, they were the only people I felt comfortable talking to about my problem, but they never seemed to accurately comprehend the severity of my struggle.

One day, the travel agency decided that it was time to relocate the business, and they asked me to paint the new building. On the second day of painting, I needed to go downtown to get some supplies. On the way down the mountain toward Colorado Springs, a voice spoke to me. It was a voice that I knew well. The whispers of this unseen evil taunted, "You have some money. Why not take one hit?" I tried to push the temptation aside, but it persisted. "One hit will surely not end the world, and you deserve it, for you have not enjoyed the feelings of being high for a long time." I tried to ignore the desires of my flesh.

Walking through the aisles of Wal-Mart, I ran into a girl whom I had met a few months earlier. She asked me how I was doing, showed a genuine kindness, and said, "So, do you want to come and party with me tonight?" At this point, I felt a strong pull on my heart that said, "RUN. Run as fast as you can to the nearest phone and call your boss." But I ignored the prompting and instead said, "Sure, I have nothing going on tonight."

I ended up at her house with a group that resembled the one I had so adamantly left behind by moving to Colorado. Nothing good could come from this predicament. Once again, I heard the Spirit say, "Run, this is not a place to be lounging about."

As I drank the afternoon away, more hurting and lost young people showed up for the party, and soon I was beyond my faculties. The orgy of sex, drugs, and alcohol consumed me, and the party continued long into the next day. By the end of the second day, I was longing for my drug of choice—crack. I asked if anyone knew where I might find some. No one was much help. The girl from Wal-Mart solicited a crowd to go dancing, so I went with them.

We went to a club on Cimarron Street, and there I met a dealer. I'll refer to her as Kelly. Kelly provided us with weed and other drugs. I asked if she had any crack, and she did.

At the end of that night, I left with Kelly, and she took me to a rundown Victorian house on the west side of the downtown area. Days passed, and I spent all my money on crack. Kelly was in and out often, but I remained with the others at the crack house doing drugs. When I had spent my last dollar, I negotiated with Kelly for more. If she would give me $50's worth of crack, she could have my cell phone until I had the money to pay her back.

As I inhaled the last of my crack, I remember lying down on a bed. The next thing I knew, I awoke to see a colleague from the travel agency standing over me, saying, "Cm'on, let's get out of here." I felt an overwhelming sense of relief. I could not comprehend how in the world he had found me.

I was dazed and bewildered, but resolved to find my belongings and get out. Nathan and I left the crack house. The next day Nathan told me the whole story about how God had rescued me from total hopelessness.

What you hold in your hands is the true account of how God saved *him* from total hopelessness.

—Jeremy Barnett

By Nathan Schnackenberg:

Like the wind, visions, power encounters, and undeniable moves of God's Holy Spirit come from directions and at times that we often do not expect. Such was the case for me on that Saturday night. I had a few friends over to my home to pray for Jeremy, a friend of ours, who had been missing for a few days, most likely suffering under the bondage of a relentless crack cocaine addiction. It was late, probably 11:30 p.m. as the group was getting underway. The phone rang; it was my boss, Tim.

"Nate," he said, "I think God has shown us the way to Jeremy." I listened to Tim as he told me the story of how, for no apparent reason, about fifteen minutes earlier he had gotten himself out of bed, put his clothes on, and drove to the office. "I just felt as though Jeremy might be trying to get into the office to steal stuff in order to continue paying for whatever he's doing right now" was Tim's reasoning. As he arrived at the office, he checked the door, and all was well. Not satisfied, Tim unlocked the office, disarmed the automatic alarm system, and began to look around. The place was in order.

The phone rang right at that moment; as Tim checked the caller ID, he realized that it was Jeremy's cell phone number. Tim quickly answered, "Hello, Jeremy?" Dead silence on the other end. "Hello, Jeremy, are you there?" More silence.

Just as Tim was about to hang up, he heard it, and his heart jumped. The sound of faint laughing and talking on the other end. Then rap music boomed. Tim attempted again, "Hello, Jeremy, are you there?" No answer. Evidently, the phone was connected to Tim at that very moment, but those on the other end had no idea.

Five or so minutes later, the phone went dead, and Tim frantically called back, hoping beyond hope that someone would answer. A woman did. Tim asked to speak to Jeremy, but the woman's reply was, "I'm sorry, he's not here."

Tim thought quickly and responded with, "That sucks because I was going to ask him to score me some drugs." The plan worked. The woman eagerly told Tim, "Well, I can get you drugs if that's what you're after."

The woman told Tim where to meet her, and Tim called my house. Our conversation hit a lull as Tim asked, "So, what should we do?"

"I think we should go and get him," was my reply, and we decided that I would come and pick Tim up at the office on our way down the pass to Colorado Springs.

I told the other group members what had just happened, and we quickly got into a circle and prayed, thanking the Lord for this opportunity. For roughly four days straight, we had been trying Jeremy's cell phone relentlessly, but not once were we able to get through. Suddenly now, as Tim arbitrarily woke up, went to the office, and through a chance phone call whereby the phone dialed itself ... no, we were sure that God was intimately involved in the rescue of our friend from the grip of a spirit of addiction.

My friend Scott offered to drive; the others remained behind and continued to pray for us. Scott drove down Highway 24, roughly twenty miles to Colorado Springs. The drug dealer who Tim spoke to on the phone gave us directions to a club on the south side of downtown; as we arrived, we realized it was a hip-hop club. After we parked, we sat in the car waiting, wondering what to do next. "Jeremy's white, so he should stick out here. Let's go in and take a look" was one suggestion, and it seemed good, so we walked into the club. It was about 12:15 a.m.

No Jeremy was to be found. Tim decided to dial the cell phone back, and once again, the woman answered the phone. Tim told her where we were, and she assured us that she was on her way and gave us the description of her vehicle. A yellow Buick. We decided that Scott and Tim would wait in Scott's car while I negotiated with the woman to take us to where Jeremy was.

It was a cold night. The bass coming from the music inside the club added to my nervousness as I stood alone on the curb, waiting for a yellow Buick to pull up. Finally it did. I got into the car and began to talk to the woman as she pulled out her stash of drugs.

"Put those away. I did not come here for drugs," I began. She looked at me coldly, almost agitated.

"Then why the h--- did you call me?" she shot back.

"Because I need to find the person who owns that phone."

"Well, you're looking at her," she cut me off. "That junkie owed me money. He's lucky I chose to take this phone and not his skin!"

"Take me to him," I said, this time lowering my tone.

"I can't," she said plainly.

"Why not?"

"You can't go where he is, fool, and I can't take you there."

"So you know where he is?"

"I can't take you there, so get out of my car," she said, and looked out of her driver-side window to motion for one of the club bouncers to come over and help remove me from the vehicle.

"Someone is trying to kill him," I said, without much thought. She put a hand up and waved the bouncer away.

"Who?" she asked, intrigued.

"Satan, who else? You know this lifestyle will kill him if he doesn't get help," I said.

"So, who the h--- are you?" she asked, somewhat mockingly.

"I'm sent by God." A simple, very direct retort.

The car was silent as she sat, fidgeting with her key chain dangling above her right knee. After a minute or two, she looked at me and asked, "What will I get out of this? If I do this for you, I'm risking my own neck."

"You'll get the satisfaction of knowing that you helped save a life," I said, but sensing that such a comment would hold little to no weight, I added, "And I'll pay you for your time." She perked up as I showed her my money clip and the wad of cash I had on me.

"Fine, I'll take you," she said, as she leaned out of her window to tell her entourage that she would catch up with them later. Just as she did so, I pulled roughly $160 off the clip and put it into another pocket. This coked-up, drunk woman would never know …

She drove through downtown, and I found myself getting frazzled when she almost rear-ended a police vehicle. She laughed it off, but I yelled at her. She told me to calm down and "be cool."

Finally, we found ourselves in a dark neighborhood; dim streetlights lit small cylinders of illumination every fifty yards. Jeremy's car was parked on the curb in front of a very old and rundown Victorian-style home. It had a large front porch. The fence was gone in some places, and the yard was in disarray. The steps creaked as we walked onto the porch and up to the front door. No lights could be seen, but a TV was on in a room just inside the front door.

The woman knocked repeatedly as Tim and Scott drove up, parking their vehicle on the curb in front of the woman's yellow Buick. They remained in the vehicle, no doubt praying for Jeremy and me.

She knocked again, then looked at me and said, "You know they will never let you in this place; they don't know you. This is a stupid idea." She knocked again, still no answer.

"Go stand over there," she said, pointing to the corner of the patio and out of sight. I followed her directions, and no sooner did I do that, then the door swung open, and a big black man said, "Kelly, what do you want?"

"Well, we're here for the white kid," she said, trembling.

"Who's 'we,'" came the reply, and I decided to go and meet this guy head-on. I walked into sight and looked him straight in the eyes. "We are here for him," I said.

The man simply moved out of my way, holding the door open for me with one hand and giving me the "after you" gesture with the other. I kept eye contact with him, as he seemed to shrink in stature as I walked by. Kelly followed.

I looked at the man after I was inside the house, and he pointed upstairs, so I turned and began the ascent. One boy, who looked to be about fourteen years old, was sitting on the steps about a third of the way up, smoking something. We passed him, but he did not look at us. As I approached the top landing of the staircase, I was startled by the sudden appearance of a young man, shirtless, standing in only his boxers, who whipped around the corner and blocked my way. He had one hand on the railing and the other palm against the wall. I looked at him, and he sneered at me. It was as though his face contorted ever so slightly. I looked him in the eyes, searching for something to say to him. Instead, I thought to myself, "Get out of the way."

No sooner did I think those words, then he flew backward, levitated a few inches, and was thrust, or smashed up, against the wall behind him. He literally flew with unseen force straight backward, away from me, and into the wall behind him. His arms were stretched out, as if in the crucifix position. His wrists were firmly stuck to the wall, but his fingers and hands were flexing, as if he were trying to get free. His neck then stretched and became long, and his face jerked in one single motion to a place where his left cheek was affixed to the wall. His hands quit flexing, and sheer panic became his facial expression as his beady eyes fixed themselves on me in a desperate plea for help. He could not move, or he dared not. His feet hit the wall one last time, and I looked to see that he was indeed not standing on the ground. He was off the ground by about an inch or two, but his feet were firm, and his ankles seemed to be glued to the wall similarly to the way his wrists were. He breathed heavily as I turned and looked at Kelly, who watched in amazement. I said to her, "The Spirit of the Lord has entered this place."

Rounding a corner, we found Jeremy under a heap of tattered blankets on an old mattress. There were two men smoking cigarettes in the room on the far end, and as I entered, they crouched low together, squatted down, put their heads down, and didn't look up at me. I began attempting to rouse Jeremy when I heard a scream from another room. I noticed a doorway in the back of the room in which Jeremy was sleeping, and from that door a woman briskly walked toward me, screaming.

"I know who you are. I'll kill you for this. I know who you are, and he's mine. You can't have him, he's mine! Get the f--- out of here, he's mine." On and on the woman screamed, in an awful screech. She then lunged at me, holding a butcher's knife in her left hand, saying, "I'll cut you for this!"

As she lunged toward me, Kelly sideswiped the woman from my right, pushing the attacker down. The attacker hit her head on the bed frame and was knocked out as Kelly yelled, "No, stop this!" There was silence, then Kelly continued saying, "Stop this, stop …" As she turned to look at me, she had tears streaming down her face, and she said, "Because we're saving a life today, aren't we?"

I looked at her and said, "Yes, Kelly, we are saving a life today. From this day forward, why not commit yourself to saving lives instead of helping the enemy take them?" And with that, she lost it. She fell into the fetal position and cried bitterly, just inside the doorway of this little room. I looked around. One crack dealer crying in the fetal position, my friend passed out on an old bed, two little pathetic men squatting together in a corner, refusing to look in my direction, and one voodoo priestess knocked out on the floor beside the bed. It was quite a sight.

I tapped Jeremy on the foot and woke him. He looked at me, shock in his eyes. I said, "Come on, brother, it is time for you to leave this place." He began to say, "How …" and I cut him off, saying, "I'll explain it later. Get your stuff and let's go, now."

He put his glasses on and began to gather his belongings when the witch woke up. "Hurry, Jeremy," I said. The witch began to rock herself, chanting in a language I did not understand. She was sitting, knees up, rocking and chanting. Jeremy got distracted. "Hurry, Jeremy, we need to go, bro." Then she started again, "I know who you are. Get out or I will kill you!"

"Your threats are empty. Shut up!" I said, pointing directly at her. "Quickly, Jeremy, let's go," I encouraged him to keep moving. The woman got to her feet and flung herself over Jeremy, inhibiting his movement, not allowing him to put his socks on. "You can't have him," she began to scream again.

"Get off of him," I told the woman over and over. She would not. Finally, I grasped the woman by her left shoulder and threw her off Jeremy. She staggered backward. I pointed directly at her and said, "Knock it off. Don't touch him again. Do you understand?" The spiritual battle was intense for, even at that moment, I knew that it was not me, Nathan, speaking those words to this woman. Rather, the Spirit of the Lord in me was speaking those words to the spirit of witchcraft in her. It was a wild scene.

She then noticed the knife that she had dropped earlier. She lunged for it and picked it up. The threats continued, and I was at a loss for what to do. As she came near, knife in hand, eyes wild and red, screaming and cursing and chanting, I made an unexpected decision. I looked at the woman, and I mouthed this sentence. It was not audible, but I said, "Stop! I am here for him, and I will leave with him. Right now, you will turn and you will walk away from me in the name of Jesus Christ."

When I was mid-sentence, this woman stopped, attempted one last time to get a word out but couldn't, and stammered instead. The arm carrying the knife went limp, her shoulders shrugged, and she turned and walked straight out of the room without another word. Jeremy got his stuff, and we were on our way out.

Reaching the staircase, Jeremy stopped and did a double take in the direction of the wall. "What's this?" he managed, gesturing toward the shirtless man plastered in a crucifix position up against the wall, sheer panic in his eyes. "I'll tell you all about it tomorrow, bro. Let's go." We drove back to Woodland Park in silence. Jeremy's father came to my house at roughly 2:00 a.m. crying tears of joy. Jeremy has since kicked the habit.

That story is true. So is this book. It's a raw and real portrayal of my life: the childhood pain, the youthful rebellion, and the redemption through Christ that I have experienced. I am the prodigal son. This book tells the stories of how I came to follow the pathway to abandon.

—Nathan Schnackenberg

BIRTH PAINS
OF A NEW LIFE

The time of life when I really started to think critically about my past and recall the painful memories of old, relive them, and receive healing through Jesus Christ came just after I found myself entrenched in the pit of despair. I was utterly lost and without hope when I finally decided to turn my broken body around and begin walking back toward the God that I had left years earlier.

Little did I know when I began to seek His kingdom again that I was the very individual Jesus had referred to in one of His parables. I am the prodigal son ...

My memories of growing up in Japan are gloomy at best, downright ghastly at worst. Childhood was one of the most confusing and frustrating times of my life. I spent twelve of my first fourteen years of existence submerged in the Japanese culture and customs. I attended a Japanese public school from first through sixth grade. There were 1,400 students who attended my elementary school called Kawadaira. Besides my younger brother,

Andy, who followed me through school, I was the only full-time foreign student. The exclusion mentality of my peers became my definition of racism. My blond hair and blue eyes stuck out like a sore thumb in an ocean of dark-haired and dark-eyed students and faculty.

My family moved back and forth between Japan and America from 1979 to 1986. In 1981, my brother was born in Tokyo, but I was too young to remember. My memories begin some time later when we lived in a suburb of Tokyo called Chio da Machi. I recall the little home we lived in, the many times my family went to the neighbor's home for tea, and the many temples. It was a traditional culture in a congested city of more than 20 million people.

Other, clearer memories begin in America sometime around 1985. I remember Donaldson Elementary School in Tucson, Arizona. I remember the Foothills Mall, one of our family hangouts. I remember the heat and the smell of rain on the sandy desert floor. I loved Tucson. I have nothing but fond memories of the small but homey apartment where we lived and the Chevy Nova we drove—though my skin would stick to the vinyl seats during the summer.

In 1986, my parents accepted a long-term assignment to Japan. We relocated to Sendai, a city more than one hundred miles north of Tokyo. After a few months, my folks found a house to rent. It came with a small driveway, a medium-sized front yard and a tiny yard along the side of the house. It was a two-story home with a few rooms dedicated to the traditional Japanese tatami flooring, and other rooms designed in Western fashion with a thin carpet. There was a main bathroom downstairs and a smaller one upstairs. It was a lot bigger than our little apartment in Tucson, and I grew very fond of it.

It was time for me to start school at Kawadaira. Though my family had lived in Japan before and I had attended Japanese preschool, I had little understanding of the Japanese language on the first day of grade school. (The only member of my family who was proficient enough to get by in Japanese was my father.) I was seven years old in the spring of 1986 and could have easily been placed in the second grade. But because of my lack of written and verbal Japanese skills, my parents decided to place me in the first grade, so I have always been the oldest in my class.

The memory of that first day of school begins with me walking down the wooden stairs of our new home in Sendai ...

I could smell the eggs and bacon cooking in the kitchen, and a little bit of warmth filled my heart. I was nervous—I knew it was my first day of school in a place where I hardly knew the language. Though the day was poised with difficulty, Mom sure started it off well. I ate, happy at first, and then realized that the sooner I finished my food, the sooner I would be walking out the front door on my way to this new uncertainty. After breakfast, Dad helped me gather a few things for school and said, "Are you ready to go?" I nodded slowly.

An overcast day greeted us, but the air was fresh—as fresh as the air could be in a densely populated city of more than 1 million people.

"This is the route you will need to take every day, so pay attention, OK?" Dad said, seeming oblivious to my state of mind and nervousness. I nodded, but didn't feel like talking.

It was a straight walk about one mile up a hill to the school, which was located on the left-hand side of the bendless road. We walked slowly. Dad talked, I listened— sort of. I was more concerned with trying to keep the bacon and eggs down as my stomach continued its protest against the stress of the morning. I concentrated on taking deep breaths, one after another. Before long, and much sooner

*than I might have liked, Dad interrupted my fixation on
the ground in front of my feet with, "We're here; are you
ready for this?"*

*I looked up at him with terror in my eyes and nodded.
Just then, a bell chimed loudly in the complex. "Let's hurry;
you'll be late."*

*Standing at the crosswalk, the school looked huge; the
massiveness of it caused me to do a double take. In front of
us was an impressive courtyard with two soccer goals. The
soccer field made of soft dirt ran along the long side of the
school building.*

*There was not a single plot of grass on the grounds, only
dirt and rocks. The paint on the playground equipment
was wearing away, and rust prevailed. The school
was painted gray, and the gymnasium was brown. I
remembered Donaldson (the elementary school I attended
in Tucson) having grass, color, and warmth. By contrast,
surrounding this entire complex was a chain-link fence
that gave the campus a menacing look.*

*The students were already inside. The loud chime of the
school bell had marked the beginning of classes. Dad and I
walked to one of the massive doors and almost put a poor first-
grader into cardiac arrest. The boy appeared out of nowhere.
There was a look of shock and confusion on the youngster's face,
who looked to be about my age, as he inched his way backward
staring at me and my father in disbelief and wonder. Dad
chuckled and uttered something in Japanese. His manifest reply
to Dad's kindness was to run away from us with a shriek. Dad
seemed to take no notice and continued on.*

*"This is where you take off your shoes and put on the school
slippers," he said. "We'll get you some slippers in a few days,
but for now just walk around in socks." A genkan is the front-
door location within a building or home that is designated and
reserved for this custom of removing outdoor shoes and putting*

on indoor ones. I had no idea that this tradition was prevalent in school buildings as well as in homes. Usually within a business sector of a city, one is allowed to walk into buildings with his or her shoes on.

The flooring just past the genkan was made of slick, green tile. About a minute later, it was evident that the green tiles were used throughout the entire building ... something resembling the flooring of a hospital. "Psychiatric Hospital" is what comes to mind now, as I remember the interior design of this grade school.

I was taking in a lot all at once. As I stood up with my outdoor shoes in hand, I remember thinking that the school looked as unpleasant on the inside as it had on the outside. Not like I knew what grade schools in Japan were supposed to look like, but there was no color in this building except the puke-green flooring and light gray walls. Based on my own limited experience in schools (I only had Donaldson to compare), I disliked what I saw in this Japanese institute of learning.

What happened next was so unexpected that words don't do it justice. I heard a ruckus coming from around the corner to our left. Suddenly, about fifty Japanese first-graders came around the bend and attacked me! At least it felt like an attack, as they nearly knocked me over. Before I knew what was happening, there was a ring of Japanese students around my dad and me, all yelling and screaming. I had no idea what they were saying. I put my hands over my ears at first, as I got pushed from one side to another by this mob of little kids. Hundreds of little fingers were running through my hair, grabbing at me, touching me. I slapped at the hands and tried to push them away. I managed a quick glance toward Dad, who was smiling! I wondered what on earth he was smiling at. I felt myself becoming distressed to the point of panic, as I had no idea what was going on. It felt like a bad dream.

"Quit yelling at me!" might have been what I said out loud

as I tossed a punch. "Stop touching me!" I thought as I sent a punch in another direction. Confusion continued to well up within me, when suddenly I noticed Dad making headway toward me. By now he was not smiling anymore, but physically moving away the little kids who separated us. When he got within arm's reach, I found that my personal space was quickly given back to me. This action on Dad's part eased my fear a bit.

After what seemed like a prolonged eternity, we advanced down the hall, roughly fifty feet, to a teacher who had watched this phenomenon with an offensive level of complacency. As we approached, he finally ordered the kids back to the classroom. "It's about time," I thought, as he exchanged pleasantries with us that consisted of bowing sessions followed by more of the same. I just watched.

The teacher and Dad talked as I tried to clear my mind of the past few minutes and gain my bearings. The disturbance caused by this class of unruly students had piqued the curiosity of students and teachers in other classrooms down the hall, who slowly came out into the hall to see what all the upheaval was about. They simply stood and gawked at Dad and me. As I gawked back, trying to match their insolent looks, I wondered what the big deal was. "There were kids in Tucson that looked different than me, and nobody seemed to care there." As I pondered this thought, I remember a sudden feeling of despondency came over me as a wave crashes upon a rock. I looked down the hallway toward the many faces staring at me and understood for the first time—I was the only different-looking person in this entire school. My eyes glazed over as I began to realize what a compromising situation I was being put in. "Everyone in this place is alike except me." The thought began to haunt me.

The teacher led me into the classroom and motioned for me to sit down in an empty seat located front row and center. (To this day, I hate sitting in the front of a classroom, church, *or gathering of any kind.) I sat, still in disbelief of what I had just moments ago come to realize, and I kept sitting in that chair, stiff as a board, for the rest of the day. The teacher said something in what he thought was English, but I didn't understand. I simply nodded and said "yes" to everything he said to me.*

During recess, the other kids went outside, and the teacher tried to have a conversation with me. I had no idea what he was saying. He tried to speak English, but he couldn't accomplish such a feat any more than I could speak Japanese. Slowly I felt a cloud creep over me. It felt like the beginning of the end.

In many ways, it probably was the beginning of the end. In 2001, I began to deliberately resurrect old and repressed memories of what I now call the Lost Years of my life. The Lost Years began soon after my first day at Kawadaira in 1986, where I continued to repress painful memories until I began to play soccer in 1990. I would often look at old pictures with family members, but not be able to recall, for the life of me, any circumstances surrounding those shots taken from the Lost Years. My forgetfulness never made sense, because I could clearly remember earlier times in Tokyo or Tucson. I disregarded my inability to remember life between '86 and '90 by attributing it to a very bad memory. But in my heart, I knew that was not really true.

In 2001, I came to the realization that I was lost. I had no idea who I was; I only knew the identities I allowed myself to show others. I was living at an inhuman speed, and I was fast approaching a very destructive end. I had no clue what I had undergone in the Lost Years, and I decided that it was time to take a long and painful journey back in time for the sake of rediscovery. I made attempts to remember and to re-experience. I needed to meet the real me for the first time.

I now refer to the time from 2001 to 2003 as the Years of Emergence, for it was during this period that the Lost Years were unveiled and I finally met the real me. During the Years of Emergence, I began to realize that those Lost Years in Japan were crucial and purposeful to the path that I ultimately chose to walk. I discovered that the rebellions of my adolescence were exactly what I needed before I could comprehend God's love for me as His son. The end result was the realization that I was one of many billions of people, living life to the fullest of my limited understanding, with my feet planted firmly on the pathway to abandon.

QUESTIONS
OF THE HEART

02

After hitting rock bottom physically, spiritually, emotionally, and relationally in 2001, I took a serious look at my trust issues. I wondered why I distrusted people so much. One day as I meditated on this question, I was led back to the cultural disparities between Japan and America—contrasts I had lived with for many years but had never thought about critically.

In America, children are familiar with the jingle of an ice-cream truck slowly rolling along the quiet streets of the neighborhood. In Japan, inhabitants hear the mystically strange melody of a sweet-potato cart creeping along the streets at dusk, accompanied by the distinctly beautiful aroma that begins to fill the air. In Sendai, my family got all too used to this sweet potato event. As I look back, the sound, smell, and feeling of the sweet potato truck drawing near are associated with a cool evening and smoke rising from the portable furnace that is used to cook the potatoes.

In the States, we have spas nestled in strip malls where men and women go to get pampered and enjoy a moment of peace and relaxation. In Japan, they have a similar type of getaway called *Onsen* (Oun-sen), which means "bathhouse." These Onsen facilities are normally located high on a lush volcanic mountain, nestled in a corner of natural paradise. The concept of an Onsen is the same as the concept of a spa, though the methodology of receiving this sought-after peace and relaxation is so different. Men and women go to these places to get away from the hustle of life—to reconnect mind, body, and spirit with the true essence of inner peace. On special occasions, our family went to the Onsen facilities, though they remained a luxury that we couldn't regularly afford. I am so fond of my Onsen memories …

We drove upward, through lush greenery to an ancient building ornamented in rich, Buddhist décor. A woman dressed in the traditional Japanese kimono greeted us at the door and ushered us into the main lobby. We were then handed a traditional fishing pole and bait and told to go catch our supper in one of many secluded pools of water close by. Once we caught our fill, we carried the fish back to the main building and the kitchen staff asked, "By what time should we have this supper prepared for you?" Usually, we asked for an hour or two so as to enjoy the bath. From there, Mom went one way, and Dad, Andy, and I another—to a community bath of natural volcanic sulfur water. Japanese belief holds that this water is cleansing to the body. After the bath, we dressed in a soft robe and headed up to a traditional Japanese supper of fish, rice, and soup.

There are hundreds of little cultural differences between Japan and America. Societal differences might be cause for some emotional or social shortcomings in my life, but I couldn't understand why I distrusted people the way I did. My need to know caused me to spend a lot of time thinking and writing about things in my past. But I could never figure out what had happened to lead me to this place of distrust.

One day I wrote my parents an email and asked, "Do you remember any event that sticks out in your mind regarding me between the years 1986 and 1990? Anything that may point me in a direction of realizing something that I may have forgotten?"

The email they sent back to me said,

> I remember a time, sometime after you started at Kawadaira Elementary, that a mother from the neighborhood came to our door late one afternoon. She was apologizing profusely. She got down on the cement of the genkan with her forehead to the ground, saying she was sorry. I was mystified because I could not understand why, except that it had to do with you. Her son had done something to you; I came to believe it had to do with touching you on your private parts or something to that extent. I asked you about it after she'd left. You shrugged it off saying, "Yeah, he was mean, but I hit him hard, and he fell down." I didn't really know if I should believe that or not, but you seemed cool about it.

Before I could even finish the email, I found myself lost in a very painful memory from the Lost Years. It was the first time I had recalled it, and I literally fell to the floor crying in a fit of psychological and emotional torment. I did not want to remember, but at the same time I had to.

It was the summer of '87. My class was getting ready to go out into the pool for gym class. Because I was the only different-looking kid in the school, there was generally a fond intrigue for me. But in times of changing clothes, that curiosity was channeled toward the private parts of my body. I used to change into my swimming shorts under a large oversized towel, so as to maintain some level of decency. But in a class of forty to fifty students, not everyone strove for such decency. During the previous weeks, students had begun harassing me in an attempt to get the towel off me while I was changing. So far, I had successfully managed to elude my tormentors and was hoping to make it through the summer season of pool activity.

Then one day a boy got to me in the pursuit. I was naked underneath the towel and running for my life when he caught hold of my towel and ripped it off me. Instantly, I felt fear, humiliation, despair, and hurt ... the memory is agonizingly viewed in slow motion. The entire class stopped as if the oxygen was sucked out of the room. Astonished looks and glazed eyes pierced my heart. As quickly as the oxygen was taken out, it was thrust back into the room, in a wonderful roar of laughter and excitement—they had never seen a circumcised boy before. In a panic, I looked at the classroom full of boys and girls who were hysterically laughing and pointing. Some even fell to the ground in laughter. Tears welled up in my eyes as I searched for my towel. The floor was blurry from the tears. I found the towel, covered myself, and sat in a corner. I cried and did not get up until the entire class had departed for the pool for gym class.

The memory itself was so very foreign to me that it seemed fake and far removed from my consciousness, yet so emotionally compelling. It did not take long for me to see the truth, and though I tried to deny it, this memory was a part of the difficult season I experienced in Japan. It was one in a long line of many memories that fostered the Lost Years.

By mulling over the event many times and recognizing the difference between what actually happened as opposed to what I told my mom, I realized where my distrust of people might have originated.

The remembering of this event brought more questions than answers. Why did I distrust my parents? Why did I change the truth about painful events in my past? Why had I not felt comfortable about being honest? Why did I suppress memories rather than deal with them and process them? Where was God in all of this?

Despite the questions, it was encouraging to understand a bit more about myself. The Years of Emergence started off as somewhat of a game, but through real and painful discoveries of my past, finding the lost and forgotten me became an obsession.

IDENTIFICATION

OF A SECRET WAR

03

One unintentional result of my efforts to go back and understand the Lost Years was the remembrance of supernatural events. Those miraculous events became the foundation of my understanding of Christianity. Many Christian denominations rebut the existence of supernatural healing, deliverance, and power encounters, while other denominations tend not to legitimize anything as being Christian unless it is accompanied by the supernatural. I never had much of an opinion about Christian spirituality prior to my efforts to reconnect with the past. But in recalling the events of healing that took place in my own body and life, some ambiguous truths about God became more solidified in my heart. It fostered a platform by which I grew in my relationship with the Lord.

As a child, I always had trouble hearing things. I know it was a bother to others, because my classic reply to a question or comment was a very loud "What?" I was like that annoying kid who refuses to turn the walkman headset down but insists on talking to you over the music only he hears. This issue of not hearing and replying to people a few decibels too loud was a constant problem. It was really no big deal for me, because I had never been able to hear well, so I didn't know what I was missing. What I didn't like was enduring the many ear surgeries. Sometimes I was put under by anesthesia, and other times a barbaric doctor would jab a needle through my eardrum, causing excruciating pain but no better hearing. The doctor visits were common to me. Every few months I went back in because my folks decided to give the doctors another chance to fix my hearing problem—until 1989.

One day, my mom said to me, "We are going to have a man come over to the house today and pray for your ears." I thought nothing of it at the time. I assumed that it would not be painful, so I didn't care too much.

I was in the living room when he arrived at the door with some friends. He came in and exchanged pleasantries with the family. Soon, he was crouched down and looking at me face to face. He asked me, "Do you believe that God can heal your ears?" I vividly remember my thoughts just after he asked me this. "Well, sure He can," I replied with absolute certainty. God created the heavens and the earth, so, of course, He could heal my ears! It was a no-brainer.

The man, a friend of the other missionaries stationed in Sendai, looked up at my folks and the onlookers and said, "See, that is pure and honest childlike faith!"

He sat me down on a chair and stood behind me. He placed his hands on my ears and began to pray. I prayed earnestly that God would answer the prayer for my ears. He finished the prayer simply and with "Amen" pulled his hands off my ears. Pop! A noise ricocheted inside my head, then a series of loud noises—as if someone were clapping their hands by my ears! I clasped my hands over my ears in an attempt to quiet the sound.

The man was merely snapping his fingers in the next room. He had finished the prayer and walked backward, through the kitchen, through the hallway, and into a bathroom—all the while snapping his fingers as a show of God's awesome power! I was dumbfounded. Everyone in the room was crying and shouting!

The last memory I have of this miraculous healing is of me using the restroom later that day. I finished my business and flushed the toilet as I always did, but this time, as the water flowed down the bowl, I was shocked and fell down. For a minute I didn't know what was going on. In that moment I first conceptualized that the toilet, when flushed, made a noise that seemed to be quite loud!

It was no surprise to me that God healed my ears. Based on the doctrinally sound teachings of my parents, God is love, and, in love, God gladly heals the afflicted. Not only that, but Bible stories tell of Jesus and the disciples healing people, so the fact that God healed my ears was not surprising. It was somewhat expected from a child's point of view. This act of healing only reconfirmed the truth that God can move whenever and however He chooses and that He joyfully gives good gifts to His children who believe.

My parents' eyes were suddenly opened wide to the reality of spiritual war over Japan and in their own lives after this prayer meeting and others like it, where people were healed and delivered from spiritual forces. There was a war going on for my heart and mind as well, but at the time, I was much too young to realize it. My folks, however, began to see more clearly what erects itself between the truth of salvation and the inability of the Japanese to surrender their lives to Christ. I remember having conversations with my folks about Buddhism and the spiritual war in Japan.

My mom said this:

Buddhism itself holds people in bondage to doing works that will enhance their chances or good fortunes in life. The underlying root theology is fear—of the future, of bad circumstances, and of being considered tainted, which results in ostracism. The lie is that they can influence their personal futures by doing religious-type stuff. For example, I remember going with a group of neighborhood ladies from Kawadaira (our neighborhood) on an excursion to the Nikka whiskey plant and the main Buddhist temple outside of Sendai. At the whiskey place, I had no sense of overt spiritual stuff. We hung out, sampled the apple wine, and had a good time. But I don't remember there being any display of compulsive behavior among the ladies. Then we got back onto the bus and went to the temple.

When we turned into the narrow lane that led to the temple, I felt as though the sun had gone behind a cloud, except that it was already cloudy and the weather hadn't changed. The spiritual atmosphere was dark on the temple grounds. Upon arriving at the temple, the ladies and male bus driver were suddenly compelled to rush to the incense altar, buy the sticks of incense, put them into the ashes, and wave the smoke over themselves. They waved this smoke over me, as well. This was supposed to prevent sickness. While they were frantically doing this, they told me that they didn't really believe in this ritual, but that it was just something they did by tradition. It was clear to me that they were in bondage. They couldn't *not* do it. There were the same frantic, compulsive actions in the back of the temple where everyone bought and lit a candle for good luck.

Dad had another perspective:

I believe the strongest control over the Japanese is not Buddhism but nationalism. They accept anything as long as it does not affect their being Japanese first. Thus you have the Shinto/Buddhist combination. The best of both worlds created this binding fear. When they are faced with making a decision for Christ, lordship is one of the major hurdles. No longer can being Japanese be first, but Christ must become first. Our international organization's Japanese country director at the time said, "For us Japanese, the spirit of conformity is a major stronghold." I agree, and that adds to the difficulty of nationalism. It is hard to break away without being cut off, in their culture especially.

Mom continued:

At that time in '94, Japanese young people were really diverging from the traditional social mentality and getting into New Age-type stuff. A book on *How to Effectively Curse Your Competitor* was a best seller, and books on the *Glowing Ball of Fire* and *Power of the Hand* were really popular. Our Japanese friends used horoscopes, blood-type divination, palm readers—anything to get an edge on their personal fate. The big lie, in my opinion, is their belief that life is capricious—it may be bad to you sometimes, but you can make your way better by religiously performing the sacred rituals. The mentality of an average Japanese is that of a depressed, stoic, "hard-knock" life. Another stronghold over the country is the honoring of death. Suicide is preferred instead of living in shame. Japan continues to be a world leader in suicide rates. You remember the Buddhist masks all over the place? Those masks are symbolic of the hardness of life.

As I look back on my life in Japan, it is now easier to see how one small lie can distort my understanding of God and effectively cripple an entire people group. In Japan, life is simply hard; and because life is hard, it is not a gift but a curse. If life is a curse, then the one who gave life—God—must be somewhat harsh at best, downright evil at worst.

The harshest influence that Buddhism and Japanese nationalism had on me was in the area of mandatory conformity. Japanese society demanded that all inhabitants conform to the mold of a group. I was caught between a rock and a hard place. The rock, for me, was that I could never be a part of the "group" in Japan for I was a *gaijin*, which means "outsider." The hard place was the endless pressure to conform to a group. I desperately wanted and yearned for the acceptance and comfort that the various groups had to offer, but I was always excluded. Ironically, the end of the Lost Years was the beginning of my involvement in a group—the soccer team.

P/ARTING
QUESTIONS

04

The first vivid memories I have after the Lost Years are related to playing soccer. In fourth grade I became eligible to try out for the school team, and, though I had never played before, my folks wanted me to find some hobbies that I enjoyed. I had tried piano lessons in third grade, but they did little more than bore the heck out of me. We decided that I should try out for the team and give soccer a chance. The first day of practice remains vividly clear.

I arrived late to practice that first day. Both coaches and players were utterly surprised to see me walk in. It was probably common knowledge that I generally despised school. However, the shock only lasted about three minutes. I couldn't believe it. As soon as the practice was underway, I got involved, and everyone was focused on the task at

*hand. I did not notice another single look from anyone
during that practice. Afterward, everyone calmly left, and
I went my way in disbelief. Not only did I not get harassed,
I was treated with respect, as an equal. And soccer was
actually fun!*

Life changed dramatically for the rest of elementary school. I
may have seen one or two members of the team in school, but
mostly, I had not seen these athletes before. They had their own
little group, and, by simply being on the soccer team, I was ushered
into that group and considered an equal. It was wonderful to finally
have some friends!

The relationships that I made in soccer were just what I needed,
but they never extended past the geographical boundaries of
our little suburban school district, until one day just before we
graduated and went our separate ways. A friend said, "A few of us
are going downtown to shop and eat. We were wondering if you
would like to go?" I was ecstatic. I quickly said, "Yes!" Though I had
not received permission from my parents, I made up my mind to
go. This was the breakthrough I was waiting for. I couldn't believe
that I was actually being invited to go somewhere outside the
boundaries of our little community where everyone had become
comfortable with me. My folks quickly agreed that this was a good
thing, and they gave me money for the bus and subway ride into
the downtown district.

I have a lot of good memories from that day, but my friends did
not know what they were getting themselves into by asking me to
tag along with them. Soon after we arrived downtown, they began
to notice the awkward stares and chuckles that people gave me
because I was different. It was uncomfortable for them. At one
point, they all chose to walk about twenty feet away from me so
that they could remove themselves from the ridicule. I had no real

problem with that because I hated the scorn and mocking also. If I had the chance to avoid it, I probably would have chosen to do the same thing. Regardless, this scene sent a clear message that I already understood: friendship works to the extent of mutual understanding and comfort—and not beyond.

I had been in similar situations before when the soccer team played away games. Friends would fade away when push came to shove, and the cultural ignorance of Japan set in against me. Even though I never believed my friends had my back, I was overjoyed to have these friendships, because they made my life much superior to the existence I lived during the dark years without any friends. I finally had a measure of identity and acceptance.

The day progressed, and we had fun right up to the point where it was time to catch the bus home. We were waiting at the bus station when an older gentleman came up and began to yell at me. He spoke with a very traditional dialect, and I did not understand all that he was saying—something about contaminating the purity of Japan by being there. He then tried to rally my friends against me by saying, "Don't you know he is bad? He is American, and he is bad. You do not need to be near him. You disgrace your family by associating with him." On and on the guy went, and then the most amazing thing happened. My buddies stepped between the old man and me, and they rebuked him like I had never heard a child rebuke an adult in the history of living there! The man could not compete with four young men telling him all the reasons for his flawed outlook on foreigners. They were not nice about it, either, and they resolutely said, "No, we will not stop hanging out with him because he is a good guy. You should get to know people before you judge them, or you disgrace your family." Finally he walked away. Our bus arrived soon after that, and barely a word was spoken on the ride home until we all said goodbye and headed to our homes. My friends standing up for me was a direct contradiction to my belief about friendship and the extent to which friendship could go. They showed me that friends do stand up for each other.

After I graduated from Kawadaira Elementary School, I spent seventh grade attending the local Sendai American School (SAS). This was a fun year for me. The school consisted of about twenty-five students ranging in grade levels between first and ninth grade. I quickly developed strong ties with these students. The student body represented eight to ten different nationalities, and there was a lot of acceptance and tolerance for one another. Many of the students looked to me for leadership, as I was the oldest boy in the school. This respect was so incredibly different from the belittling received from the Japanese.

One day, four kids from SAS were at my parents' home for a sleepover. We stayed up late watching TV and playing video games. One of the boys had fallen asleep, but the rest of us decided to sneak out and go walking around the town. We got dressed for the cold and left. It was about two in the morning. As we walked, our young minds instantly switched into fantasy mode and set ourselves a mission to go out and come back undetected. We dodged to stay out of view from the cars that passed; we avoided other people; and we attempted to remain silent during the entire journey, save the limited conversations we had with one another along the way.

After about forty-five minutes of walking, we were reaching the end of the Kawadaira district boundaries. We noticed a looming structure in the distance on a street that I had very seldom walked. As we drew nearer, we realized that it was a water tower. The discussion began.

"Let's climb it," one of my buddies said.

"Yeah," was my reply.

"No," said the other guy.

The debate continued until two of us decided we were brave, and the other two were content to let us be stupid. I followed my buddy up the ladder on the side of the tower. The tower itself was probably about forty to fifty feet tall. I was petrified by the time I reached the one-quarter mark. I still have no idea what prompted me to continue to climb. My hands and feet were tingling. I remember thinking that my hands were too cold to grip the metal, and they might not work, and I might fall.

Finally, I reached the top, and the adrenaline felt like it was gushing through my body. I took deep breaths, one after another, and I gained composure. My buddy said, "Wow, look at all the lights of the city," but his voice seemed distant as my eyes glazed over and I stared at the beautiful sight. There were low clouds, illuminated pinkish orange, scattered across the sky. Peaks and valleys made up the landscape, and everywhere were the twinkling lights of Sendai. The moon dipped and returned out from under the clouds as the world seemed to slow to a quiet and peaceful stop. The city was asleep, and, as the breeze hit my face and weaved its way through my hair, I remember something strange came over me.

I lost myself somewhere between joy and sadness, somewhere between reality and fantasy. A part of me had hope for my future, and another part of me was full of dismay. The questions burned in my heart as I attempted to hold back tears. The questions that raged through my mind and heart were unsolicited and completely unexpected. They seemed to come out of nowhere. They were questions I had never considered and some of which I had no answer to. They were abstract and beyond my years of understanding. They caused me to feel the pain of my life. In my heart, I cried in bitterness while starving for answers.

Who am I? Why am I here? An American caught in a life that is not his own. God, who are You? Why have You allowed the misery?

I have no place that I call "home." Are we not supposed to have a home on earth? I am not Japanese, and most people here don't like me, so I cannot call Japan my home. I am American, but I know nothing of that place, so it is not my home either. I feel like an outcast who has no place to go.

I'm like a stray dog who repeatedly has the door of rejection slammed in his face.

No girl has ever talked to me, so why do I admire and long to have one accept me? Why does my heart hurt when people ignore me, and why does it hurt worse when people can't seem not to notice me? Being different is painful.

So what is life? Is life a race to see who can get through it the fastest with the least amount of pain? People run from here to there, they do this and that, and they grow old and die. What's the point of it all? Maybe life is of greater meaning than just people and circumstances. How is my accomplishment any different, better, or worse than yours? A teacher does not care that a soccer pro is noticed for his accomplishments, and a soccer pro does not care that a teacher is noticed for her accomplishments. But might God and the devil care?

What makes up, up and what makes down, down? What makes something right and what makes something wrong? The point is, there is no right and wrong. How do I know that being in Japan is wrong when I do not know where the right place is? How does my heart know that the wrongness of here is greater than the rightness of here or there?

My deep thoughts were interrupted by the sound of an airplane high in the sky. I looked up through tear-filled eyes, and I longed to be aboard that airplane destined for a different place. While some people wanted accomplishments to hang on their wall, I only wanted a different life. The pain of confusion was enough, let alone the hurts of rejection, inadequacy, and abuse over the years. "Surely I will wake up, and this life will have been only a bad dream!"

I got ahold on my emotions as we began the slow and scary descent down the ladder. On the walk home, my mind continued to seek answers to questions I never even knew I had. I was realizing for the first time that life is strange, big, and uncertain.

As we arrived back home, fear of getting caught sneaking back into the house gripped us, and we all slid back into stealth-mode. I opened the front door, and my mom was standing there with a tired and dazed look on her face. She said, "Glad you're home; now go to bed." We never heard another word about that night.

A few months later I came home from SAS, and my folks had a big surprise for Andy and me. "We're going back to America," they said, without any warning. We usually took a furlough every three years to go back to the States for a few months to visit churches and check in with supporters. My natural question was, "How long are we going to be traveling in America before coming back to Japan?" The answer I got shocked me. "We will not be coming back. We're going to be leaving Japan for good." I was at a loss for words, but I remember jumping for joy and screaming, "Yes!" Plans were made to leave within the next three months!

Mom and Dad quickly began to give away their possessions. I remember the garage giveaway (as opposed to garage sale) they organized a few days prior to our departure. There were three or four items to which they actually affixed a suggested donation price, but the rest of our family belongings were given away. My folks were adamant about blessing others. "And when we get to America, the Lord will bless us in return," they said.

I was beside myself over this choice to give stuff away, for I thought it was bad business and not logical. I had one item that belonged to me—a mountain bike. Though my folks cautioned me, I chose to sell the mountain bike instead of giving it away. I was determined to have a little cash in my pocket for the return home. The irony is that my folks were financially blessed as a result of their choice to bless, while I struggled in the area of finances throughout my adolescent years and into young adulthood.

Before I knew it, we were at the train station awaiting a one-way train straight out of Sendai. Many friends came to the station that day to see us off. Questions continued to burn in my heart again on the train platform: "Why do I feel so sad to leave this place I've always hated? Am I never going to see these people again?" Soon the train arrived, and I got on it, along with my family, and chose never to look back. This ended the first chapter of my life.

The barrage of feelings I had about leaving Japan were temporary, as the excitement of coming to the land that I had always desired to call "home" captivated me. America was a place where the grass was green and the sky was blue, a beautiful, tranquil paradise where life would forever be perfect.

UNPLEASANT
AWAKENINGS

05

My parents' decision to move away from Japan seemed rather abrupt to me. One minute I was going about my life in Japan, coping with a much-improved, though far-from-perfect situation, and the next minute we were on the plane destined for America for good. Some years after our move home, my folks revealed to Andy and me that the decision was actually not abrupt at all. Dad credits my mom's fatigue in Japan as well as my general dislike of Japan as two of the primary reasons for our return to the States. Also, Andy and I were going to be starting high school soon, and my parents felt it important for us to bond with our primary culture (whatever that meant).

The first thing I remember about returning to America is the profound joy I felt as we taxied to a stop at the gate in L.A. I looked out of the little window of the airplane and saw the baggage crew, comprised of a black, two whites, two Asians, and a Spanish-looking woman! "Yes, I'm home!" was the message I wanted to shout to the world. In my mind, America had always been a place I loved for the acceptance and tolerance of people's differences.

I had an overwhelming sense of purpose and anticipation. My outlook on life was positive as I gazed out of the aircraft window. It had been such a long time since I had felt this joy in my heart. Dare I begin to dream again? I thought about how moving back to the States allowed me to get connected into a group of real friends, who would, hopefully, have no hang-ups, hidden agendas, or issues about who I was. I thought about how I might develop an identity other than "outsider." I envisioned having an actual relationship with guys and girls my age. I dreamed about where life might take me. I felt such joy and anticipation that nothing could ever take me down again. I felt I had run the race and now crossed the finish line.

The adjustment process from Japanese to American life, however, began as soon as we exited the aircraft. Knowing that we were all hungry. Dad led us to one of those Pizza Hut/Subway/ Burger King combination food courts to get something to eat while we waited for our connecting flight into Denver. It was like a buffet line, where you order at one end and pay at the other. As I walked through the line, a man working the stand handed me an empty cup when I asked him for a Coke. I looked at the cup, puzzled, and looked at my dad. He did not notice my confusion. I then gestured to hand it back to the man while repeating my order, "Coke, please." He shot me an annoyed look and pointed to the self-serve fountain at the end of the line. I did my best to hide my embarrassment. I then bowed in a gesture of apology for my ignorance to the man behind the counter. This only led to more embarrassment, for he looked back at me crossly, as if to say, "What's your problem, kid?"

Japan and America are so different from one another. We do things on our own in America, but in Japan, people always did everything for us. The Japanese way is conformity and community with high value placed on group identification; the American way is incongruity and segregation, with high value placed on individualism.

Pumping gas, for example, is a self-serve and at-your-leisure deal in America. My shock was immense during one furlough when my dad pulled into a gas station and asked me to pump gas while he used the restroom. In Japan, a person drives up to a gas station, and a half-dozen Japanese, all dressed in the same uniform, run to the car, stand in front of it, bow, and proceed to give your vehicle a full-service inspection while pumping the required gas. They perform this task with the fervor of a NASCAR pit crew and the professionalism of a presidential aide.

These seemingly small, yet culturally significant, facets of life are sometimes difficult to get over. A Third Culture Kid has to relearn some of the basic rituals of life when going from one culture to another. This bewildering experience creates what we call "culture shock."

Another shocker for me was beholding the sheer size of many Americans—both height and girth! Because of how big many Americans are and the lack of respect that they seemed to have for one another, I often felt scared. Coming from Japan, where the average size is small and the average person respects his neighbor unconditionally, America was an intimidating place.

These cultural differences proved not to be a big deal for me in terms of transition. Relearning the ways of specific cultural standards and expectations was not all that difficult. The element of culture shock faded within a matter of months. What was difficult for me, however, was realizing that the essence of who I had become during the previous twelve years in Japan was 80 percent Japanese and 20 percent American—if even 20 percent of me could be considered American. The way I thought, how I rationalized, how I dealt with circumstances and issues, what I enjoyed, how I dressed, how I gestured in conversation, how I talked, and how I related to people was totally Japanese. My only American aspects were my physical appearance and my very limited experience in traveling throughout America.

I began to realize how different I was during the months that

my parents traveled around Colorado in search of a home. I was
having a hard time understanding the sarcasm of the typical
American. I was getting strange looks from people when I talked.
I was made fun of for the ways I dressed, gestured, and related
to people. Though I did not know it at the time, there was an
eighteen-wheeler truck called "despair" headed straight for me,
and the estimated time of collision was set for—surprise—my
emergence into the American school system.

HOW REBELLION
IS BIRTHED

06

In the spring and summer of '93, during the search for a home, we lived with my aunt and uncle just outside Denver, and the process of adaptation continued. One significant cultural paradigm shift for me was how different American women were from Japanese women. It was surprising to me that so many American women wore next to nothing out in public. In Japan, the gender roles seemed much more clearly defined, and it was strange to see women in America yelling at men in grocery stores, shopping malls, or while walking along the street. Even stranger still was that men often put their heads down and took their scolding like whipped dogs. Everything seemed so backward. There was heavy emphasis on women's rights in the news, but I couldn't get past the onslaught of ads exploiting the female body. I was overwhelmed.

One day my folks came back to my aunt and uncle's house with good news. They had found a home in a town called Woodland Park and felt that it was perfect. The next day we drove down to take a look. Woodland Park is located twenty miles west of Colorado Springs up in the mountains. It is at 8,500 feet above sea level, and I soon realized how thin the air was.

From my perspective, our home in Woodland Park had a few advantages and a few disadvantages. For one, there was something peaceful about being nestled in trees and such natural beauty. Woodland Park enjoys all four seasons and is beautiful through them all. It was a place that I felt I would enjoy. On the other hand, I was unimpressed with the fact that Woodland Park had yet to embrace a soccer team within the school system. Though the town has changed a lot over the past decade, when we moved into this sleepy little village, there was a real Western, ignorant, patriotic feel to the town, and soccer was deemed a communist sport played by the enemy in the USSR. Little did the average Woodland Park resident probably realize that the USSR did not even exist in '93, but that is beside the point. The perspective has broadened a bit since those days, and now the school district has a soccer team it is proud of.

However, when it mattered for me, there was no team, and this posed a problem. Soccer had been the savior of my childhood, and in many respects it became my identity. The prospect of not playing soccer was a scary thought, and I put up quite a bit of resistance. In the end, I liked Woodland Park and the home so much—and because the fact that we were in America continued to keep my mind positive—I chose to stop complaining.

My folks were very supportive of my feelings and allowed me to try out for a club team in Colorado Springs. I made the team, but I decided not to continue my career in soccer, because the commute was about a half-hour each way. It seemed to be more of a hassle than it was worth. My folks were so attuned to my feelings on the matter—in fact, I suspect that if I had raised cane over the soccer dilemma—they probably would have chosen not to move to Woodland Park. Finally, I chose to try other sports and make the best of an already positive-looking situation of life in America.

A few months after we moved to Woodland Park, the school year began. I was entering eighth grade, and Andy was going into sixth grade. The town had recently finished a brand-new middle school building that both Andy and I attended. As my first day of school in America drew near, my anxiety grew as well. I was excited about being in a school with boys and girls who looked the same as me, and I looked forward to making friends and being able to completely understand and communicate with everyone. And before I knew it, that first day of school was here.

My first stressor of the day was trying to get my locker opened. In Japan, there was never a need for lockers, as people generally respected the belongings of others. However, in the wonderful country of America, it was quite evident that teaching children not to steal was way too much work, and simply locking things up was a better solution. I finally figured it out and found my first class. In contrast to my first day of school at Kawadaira, my first day of school in Woodland Park was calm and somewhat relaxing. My peers ignored me, for the most part, and I relished the fact that I was not the center of attention.

But as the days and weeks passed, my odd behavior made me the topic of conversation. The differences between me and everyone else were numerous and very distinguishable. One difference was the way I gestured. If I wanted someone to come to me, I always gestured with the palm of my hand down, in a downward pulling motion. This motion didn't mean anything to the kids in America, but I was frustrated when it was ignored. Once they realized I wanted them to come to me, they made fun of it, but the habit was still hard to break. Another gesture was how I referred to myself. In America, they refer to themselves by pointing to their chests. In Japan, they point directly at their noses when referring to themselves in conversation, so I naturally did the Japanese motion ... and, boy, did that cause laughter on numerous occasions.

"You talk funny," was a comment I often heard. I had a difficult time pronouncing the "r" sound in English. For example, I pronounced the word "railroad" like this—wailwoud. The Japanese do not have the "r" sound in their language, so I had never learned to properly pronounce it. The kids poked so much fun at me for my inability to talk properly, since I looked like I should be able to, that I spent hours standing in front of my bathroom mirror practicing the sounds I couldn't say.

I had an extremely limited vocabulary, especially as it related to adolescent slang and swear words. For the first six months, I picked up new and unusual words continuously, but I never knew what to do with them. I had a feeling that the words I was hearing were not words I wanted to say in front of my parents, but I didn't know what many of them meant. I was in a dilemma: I felt I couldn't ask a peer what they meant or I would be made fun of, but I couldn't ask my folks what the words meant, as I assumed they might get mad that I said a word I shouldn't have.

During the first year that we were in the States, Andy and I spoke a language that was all our own. It was a Japanese-English fusion where our minds put sentences together combining both languages. Numerous times in school during that first year, I accidentally spoke my fusion language, and kids roared in laughter because, for all they knew, I sounded demonized. Many years later I realized that this fusion language was a blessing and a real gift. But back then, it was a curse and a wall that prohibited my advancement in American society.

The way I related to people was another point of difficulty. In Japan, people use humor, but it is a much more corny than what Americans use. In America, the sarcastic humor has very much an in-your-face and laugh-at-the-expense-of-someone-else flavor. The contrast between these two societal humor preferences created a chasm between others and me—I could not understand their humor nor could they understand mine. To my peers, I was rigid. To me, they all seemed mean. In many ways, we were both right in our perspectives of one another.

My mom tells a story of one experience she had in Japan of

trying to relate to the neighborhood Japanese women. Some of the neighborhood women had come over for tea, and it was raining outside. My mom attempted to bring some humor to the conversation by saying (in Japanese, of course), "Wow, there is so much rain outside it is as though Nojiri Lake is here in the yard!" The women, one by one, looked at each other and discussed this point. "No, Nojiri Lake is not here. What does she mean?" Another then said, "Yes, well there is a lot of rain, but not enough to fill a lake." On and on the women went, trying to analyze the sarcastic flavor of an American. In the same way, I simply couldn't relate to American humor very well that first year.

Another thing I had to adjust to was the utter chaos found in the average American classroom. Let me attempt to put it into perspective. One day in Japan, when I was in the sixth grade, I was talking to some of my buddies just before class. I was sitting on a cabinet when the teacher walked into the room. He walked straight over to me and reprimanded me for sitting on the cabinet. He turned beet-red and screamed at me for bringing the "American culture of sloppy defiance" to the school. He was absolutely livid because disrespecting the school was culturally taboo. There was never a whisper to be heard in the Japanese classroom when the teacher was lecturing.

The environment in the Japanese school is stoic at best, downright dejected at worst. It is a classic representation of Buddhism, which emphasizes the hardness of life and suffering and honors the death and rebirth processes of the life cycle—death to the child's desires to be a kid and play, and birth to the higher identity of being a student. The school environment in Japan is 180 degrees different from that of America.

I was shocked and fearful in America at the first sight of pencils and papers flying across the room, kids screaming, chairs being tossed, blatant disrespect of the teacher, and overall contempt for everyone and everything. Humanism, in its essence, venerates the individual's licentious desires, seeks to fill any and all lusts of the flesh, and tolerates this horrific cycle to an unhealthy level. To be honest, neither the Japanese nor the American school atmosphere is totally correct, but what it has become in the American secular school system is outrageous.

Relationally, I had a very arduous time getting to know guys and girls, but especially girls. There is a strange and fond attachment to the "new kid" in school. It often seems that the girls like the new guy, and the guys like the new girl before the new peer finds identity within his or her gender-specific groups. The girls in my class didn't disappoint, but I felt like a fish out of water because I had never really even talked to a girl my age before. The limited conversations I had with my female cousins represented all of my personal history in dealing with girls. I was often called "gay" by the kids (one day I finally figured out what gay meant) because of my inability to deal with some of the girls who supposedly liked me. My eighth grade year was comprised of a mess of the classic teenybopper, trying-to-be-cool American crap, and it just about ate me alive.

Due to some of these cardinal differences between the other kids and me, it was easy to become quiet and more isolated. The realization that America was not the tranquil "happy place" my hurting mind had imagined was depressing, but depression was not the reason for my isolation. Rather, I became quiet so I could concentrate on others and learn how to be an American, as well as avoid the continuous teasing and harassment.

I was committed to nonviolent ways of dealing with problems for about a year after returning to America. For one, I was scared to death because Americans were, on average, much bigger than Japanese, and I was intimidated. Secondly, I reasoned that I was in a country where I looked like everyone else, so there should be no reason to fight. Up until that time, fighting in Japanese school was only initiated out of perceived necessity. I didn't like to fight all that much, and I enjoyed those last two fight-free years in Japan. However, the temptation to resolve my issues with people physically was present in American school, as well. There were a few kids among the more rebellious in my grade who always wanted to beat me up. They never gave me a reason, but one said, "Hey, I'm going to kick your a--. What are you going to do about it?" I ended up fighting this kid when we were freshmen in high school, but during eighth grade, I always walked away.

My life in eighth grade went from exciting and new to painful and difficult as I hustled to catch up with where everyone else was emotionally, relationally, and scholastically. It seemed that no matter what I did in my life, I could not shake the fact that I was always different. No amount of conforming on my part could ever bridge the gap between others and me. It was about this time when I began to cognitively delete God out of my potential solution-to-pain weapon base. If I was hurting, there became less of a need to go to God in prayer and more of a need to fix the problem on my own. If I needed something, I didn't say, "I'll pray for it," anymore. I sought solutions to my problems through my own means, rather than exercising faith in the Lord. Pain began to win the war of my heart. I lost my faith in God's ability to protect me from hurt.

Until then, I lived by a firm set of ethics and values as any child raised by loving parents can understand. However, as I began to lose faith in God's supposed love and care for me, I questioned the level of morality that my parents chose to live by and wondered if it could actually work for me. I knew that God's Word in regard to values and ethics was: don't have sex before marriage, don't do drugs, don't cheat, don't steal, don't lie. To that extent, there was really no question in my mind. During eighth grade and even into early high school, I remained sure that I would not cross the lines that my parents had so clearly drawn for me. However, slowly these values were laid down as one compromise led to another. If only I had known that a few years later I would be wrapped up in crime, deceit, lust, violence, and greed, I might not have taken so many matters into my own hands as an eighth-grader.

Another reason I questioned the established ethics and morality in my life was due to my ever-changing and distorted perspective of pain. Somewhere between my conscious reality and the dream of a happy place, somewhere between the pain of Japan and the harshness of America, somewhere between my unyielding attempt to be accepted and never meeting the expectations of my peers, my heart became hardened. I saw life in a fuzzy haze, and it seemed to become more gray. There was less excitement and more dread. I dreamed less and became more mundane in my day-to-day functioning. What was the use of dreams, ambitions, hopes, and passion? As pain was winning the war for my heart, I entered the club of the masses called "hurting world." I suspect that nearly all of us are, or were at one time, members of this club.

Another aspect of school that overwhelmed me were the sexual temptations, peer pressure, drugs, alcohol, and vandalism. It seemed there was an unseen force that drove me into evil or compromising situations. The girls in eighth grade dressed skimpily to attract the eyes of the guys. The guys were all competing to see who could get the girls to do the most sexually explicit act. Some of my more pioneering peers found pride in raiding their parents' marijuana stash. They were always overjoyed to make a buck or two off the more daring and bold kids who lobbied for smoking pot.

At that age everyone is scared to death that "if so-and-so does this, then I have to do it too, because, if not, I'll be labeled a such-and-such." Honestly, at the end of the day, no one really cared too much about whether or not I chose to take part in value-compromising acts. But the fear of my prevailing identity (or lack of it) continued to drive the pressures of the dark and dangerous battlefield I came to know as school.

Hurting kids searching earnestly for an identity that they might call their own fueled the madness. In this humanistic society, we find more bad stuff at earlier ages with every ensuing generation. When I was in eighth grade, there were rumors of sexual acts that this girl or that guy had engaged in, but nothing was ever out in the open until high school. Now preteens in middle schools across America are shamelessly gloating about their sexual escapades. We have only evolved one decade since I was personally experiencing what I thought were overwhelming pressures in school.

Coming from Japan, I was shocked and scared during my first year at an American public school. Because I was so different, conforming to the expectations of others became a battle in which I did not have to take part as much as others. My obvious differences gave me less of a need to get high, have sex, or vandalize things. I did not suffer the pressures of my peers as much as many of the other kids did, for I was so discouraged about being different that conforming to their expectations seemed nearly impossible. In eighth grade, I began to compromise my values in the quiet place before God. I prayed less, cared about the things of Christ less, and talked about God less. This emotional distancing from my Creator marked the beginning of my season of rebellion.

THE PAIN
THAT FEEDS
REBELLION

07

As I continued to grow and learn the American way, my parents spent a few years getting their feet back on solid ground. During this reclamation to life in the States, the Lord led them into a work that was surprisingly different from the life they led as missionaries to Japan. At the time, this work was indeed radical by most Christian standards. My folks were affiliated with two separate and distinct overseas mission organizations while living in Japan. Upon returning to the States, they were led into the ministry of deliverance. One of these two organizations outrightly rejected the very thought of demons and exorcisms, and the other organization, with utter caution and skepticism, allowed them to proceed.

Deliverance, in my personal opinion, is a very biblical concept that the apostles and Jesus Himself engaged in. When I first learned of this new direction that my parents decided to pursue, I remember feelings of fear and skepticism bubbled to the surface at the very thought of exorcising demons. However, due to what we saw in Japan, there was absolutely no debating the certainty of the cosmic spiritual conflict that the Apostle Paul refers to in the book of Ephesians. Both my folks spoke in tongues and were coming out of an unexplainable spiritual battle that was directly associated with living in Japan. The Lord used their experiences in spiritual battle to birth the ministry of deliverance once they returned to America. Slowly I began to believe in their calling, though it was a far cry from anything I wanted to be associated with.

My parents' deliverance ministry matured over many years, and they have told me many captivating stories. In my heart of hearts, I always felt I had some strange and uncompromisingly compulsive desires toward evil. Back in the mid-1990s, I never wanted to admit that I might have a need to go deep with my folks. So I looked away and was content to pretend that my life was free of any evil powers and principalities. While I attended high school, I found their deliverance ministry mostly "strange," and I chose not to talk about it much. While my folks were following new paths for the Lord, I began to ask the predominant questions of my adolescent life: What is right? What is wrong? What is God?

It's evident that our society often makes a correlation between adolescence and rebellion. There seems to be an overwhelming majority of kids who rebel, to one extent or another, sometime between their middle school years and their early twenties. Our society does its part in supporting this trend by giving cute names to the blatant acts of rebelling against heartfelt dos and don'ts. Being promiscuous and spreading all sorts of sexually transmitted diseases is called "sowing wild oats." Father figures these days are more often giving high-fives for news of their son's sexual endeavors, instead of sitting down with them and explaining the physical, emotional, and spiritual dangers of promiscuity. Doing drugs is written off as an acceptable and natural facet of growing up, and is referred to as "dabbling" or "experimenting." Our society has chosen to proclaim that abortion is not only an acceptable way out of pregnancy, but also a responsible one—by killing a life, we are doing the unborn baby a favor. Our humanistic society only plays one part of the overall phenomenon of adolescent rebellion. Other parts are played in the natural, physical, emotional, and psychological changes taking place during these critical years.

Physical changes played a huge part in the stress of my adolescent years and fostered an atmosphere conducive to the birth of rebellion. Because I was one of the older students in my class, when I turned sixteen and got my license, there was overwhelming pressure to be everyone's personal driver. People who had hardly acknowledged me before began to come out of the woodwork and act like my friends, because they wanted me to give them a ride somewhere. I had to start working to pay for the car and for the gas needed to get around, so the stress of work weighed on me. Also during this season, the girls began to transform into young women, and I felt the desire to engage in relationships with them.

Emotionally, I felt burdened by the expectations of society, my peers, and my family. I was overwhelmed with the idea that I had to make good grades, figure out my life's calling, and try to be there for others in their struggles. I was preoccupied with manifesting an identity—not who I was, but who I thought everyone else wanted to see. I continued to hunger for the affirmation of my peers; I wanted to be right, straight, popular, and well liked. The pressures were enormous for me back in the '90s going to high school, and I cannot even begin to imagine what it's like for students of this new generation!

Rebellion is something we all engage in to one extent or another. It is also very unique, because one could rebel openly and violently to the extreme of committing murder while another rebels emotionally against a spouse. Both are wrong and both hurt people, but they are very different in nature. I see my personal rebellion, as well as the corporate rebellions of our world, as the product of a skewed pain perspective. If my perspective of pain is, "I feel pain, so this world owes me compensation or relief for my pain," rebellion becomes an acceptable means of showing my dissatisfaction with life when I realize that this world will not meet me where I need it to. I cannot count on a rebellious and fallen earth, or its inhabitants, to satisfy the pain of living this sin-ridden life. As long as my pain perspective is that somewhere, someone, or something upon earth will satisfy the longings of my heart, I'm doomed to more pain and further distortion. But during high school, as I searched for relief of past and current pain, faced societal and peer pressures, and neurotically attempted to define an identity for myself, truth was clouded under the confusion of my prevailing pain perspective.

My personal rebellion began in the quiet and largely unnoticeable places of my relationship with Christ. Leaving a place of childlike faith and moving into a world where man is expected to control his own destiny is the beginning of a significant rebellion that this world calls "growing up." I was not only pressured to begin the process by shedding the stupidity and ignorance of faith in exchange for scientific knowledge, but I felt vindicated for recklessly pursuing this worldly wisdom and conforming to the societal norm. At the time, I didn't know that it was all a big lie. By not praying for forgiveness and help in times of need, I compromised more than anything this world could ever offer me in the areas of security, happiness, and contentment. I exchanged my belief in the Lord's ability to completely satisfy me for the belief that I could create my own world outside of Him and be satisfied.

I am convinced that rebellion does not exist outside of a skewed perspective of God, that rebellion does not exist without pain. Through the process of being hurt as a child, I saw life through the lens of pain; thus, the pain perspective played the primary role in my process of rebellion.

My rebellion started in a seemingly inconsequential decision I made to distance myself from the Lord. Though this little compromise seemed small at the time, it ultimately fostered more pain, hurt, confusion, and misunderstandings than any other decision I have ever made. I believed that God could not help ease my pain because the distorted view I had of my past showed me that He never did before. I decided that relief would only come by my own efforts. First, I premeditatedly did not take my hurts to Him in prayer. Next, I emotionally distrusted the people around me—friends, teachers, and family members. Anyone who had the ability to potentially help ease my hurts became someone not to trust. I became very shallow in my conversations with others about heart-issues, and I emotionally distanced myself from people throughout my adolescent years.

Later in my life, this rebellion grew into overt forms of sin with the compromise of larger values in areas of drugs, alcohol, sex, and illegal temptations. In my case, high school was a time of compromising my beliefs of right and wrong for the sake of the positive affirmation others showed me. It progressed from an emotional rebellion of sitting by and allowing my friends to bad-mouth my brother to an actual rebellion, when I smoked marijuana with a group of guys. It started as an emotional rebellion of standing by while the guys talked about the girls in perverse ways and became an actual rebellion when I talked about girls in that way myself.

I saw the beginning forms of fearlessness manifested in little choices I made—like looking the other way while friends skipped school or driving the getaway car for friends who vandalized others' property. It morphed into more blatant forms of rebellion when I, too, chose to skip school with them.

Toward the middle of my high school career, I was working hard to seal my identity as a jock. Through playing football and an array of other sports, I was developing a reputation for being an athletic guy with an ability to help our team win games. This positive affirmation I received from coaches, teachers, and other athletes became a foundation that I used to create my identity as an athlete in the school. I found wonderful benefits in having this group available to help nurture my identity process.

I understand why kids choose to join a gang. The gang offers a place to develop a person's identity, just as my group of jocks offered me. The jocks in my high school were like any other peer group; they would stick up for one another in times of conflict. We ate together, went out on the town together, and associated with the same girls. We won or lost games as a group, and we all rebelled as a group. I found legitimacy in acts of rebellion; and this group fostered my emerging identity.

During this season of life, I began to seal my identity by wearing the masks of competence, strength, perfection, and fearlessness. I chose to remain lost and confused in the cycle of our created order. God slowly became a distant reality as I took matters into my own hands. It was a terribly confusing time of life for me, and one that continued on a downward spiral for years. Eventually I realized that each compromise of my values made the next compromise a little easier. And each compromise of my values drew me one step further into the world of rebellion.

TRAINING FOR
AN UNCLEAR
FUTURE

08

I met a handful of guys during eighth grade who were unusually gifted in friendship and acceptance. Two, particularly, were uncommonly nice to me and accepted me for who I was, though my speech, mannerisms, and actions differed from theirs. Dan was one of them, and about halfway through the year, we started talking about taking a short-term missions trip to another country.

I'll admit, Dan and I wanted to travel to a beach destination for a few weeks of rest and relaxation, and, in pondering possible ways to get there, a missions trip seemed to be a good and inexpensive option. Even though we were young, there were plenty of mission organizations that would accept us, so we picked one. The plan was to go to Jamaica for two weeks to help the local churches, feed the poor, comfort the dying, and encourage the local believers. There was even one day of street evangelism planned. Dan and I really had no idea what we were getting ourselves into, but we raised support, and, before we knew it, we were off to the airport.

It was an exciting time for me. Though I had traveled a lot, I had never done so without my folks, so this trip to Jamaica was a new experience. It was also my first visit to the tropics. We had a layover in Miami and met up with the rest of our group there. There were about fifteen of us traveling down to Jamaica. The layover was short, and we quickly boarded an Air Jamaica flight destined for Montego Bay. As soon as we disembarked the aircraft, we got hit with a blast of hot, sticky air, though the cloud-cover was thick. It was similar to the climate in Japan, but hotter. We got into a small bus and drove to a village called Hopewell, where we were to stay for the majority of our time in Jamaica. Wow, what a strange place it was! I had never seen such poverty. As we drove into the city limits of Hopewell, the small and rundown streets were lined with people sitting around doing nothing. Some were smoking, others were talking, and some simply sat and listened to Bob Marley on their boom boxes. It was a slow-paced life.

The bus took a right on one of the many small alley-type streets and pulled into a gated complex. The complex was an old church turned into a guesthouse, our home for the next thirteen nights. We all got off the bus, picked rooms, and headed off to an orientation meeting. The village of Hopewell smelled like a trash dump, and I found myself wondering if coming to Jamaica was a good idea. After the overview of our itinerary and daily activities, we all went back to our rooms. A container of Tang had exploded in my bag, and bugs of all sorts were having a feast. The bugs were in the bed, all over the floor, and in every crevice of my belongings. Suddenly, I knew I didn't want to be there. What I had once thought of as a vacation was fast turning into a nightmare. The lighting was dim, and it was hard to tell if we had gotten all the spiders and insects out of the room, but I finally climbed into bed hoping not to feel the hairy legs of an unwanted guest crawling on me.

Jamaica was an interesting bump in the road for me. At a time when I was defining my identity, trying to fit in with the group, and developing friendships, Dan and I decided we wanted to help the poor. Why we were moved to go, I have no idea. Part of the reason was the beautiful beaches and opportunity to travel, but there was something else. Looking back, I believe we were meant to go and experience the things we did. I remember that I felt proud to have parents who let me go on an adventure of this magnitude without the supervision of an adult (other than our trip leaders), and it allowed me to define myself as more of a risk-taker. One thing is certain: I was not ready to face the reality of poverty, and it affected my outlook on life long after I returned.

Each day we had a different set of activities planned. One day we worked in an infirmary. For the life of me, I had no idea what an infirmary was, but since I was afraid of being made fun of, I was not about to ask. I simply waited and was content to find out when we got there. We all piled into the transport beater-bus and began the trip up a gradual incline outside of Hopewell. Evidently, this infirmary was on the top of a hill somewhere, as our road continued in an incline. I was lost in thought, staring out the window, when suddenly the bus screeched to an abrupt stop. There was a lot of commotion as our group looked around to see what was going on. The bus driver leaned out of his window to ask someone what had happened, as we thought there might have been an accident. I knew that it had to be close because of how the driver had to slam on the breaks.

Finally, a man calmed down enough to tell the bus driver what was going on. He was speaking in the Jamaican dialect of English, and it was completely incomprehensible to my ear. Feeling dazed and confused, I sat and waited. Dan, who was sitting on the left side of the bus, said, "Come check this out!" I went over and peered out his window. The terrain outside was a gradual upward slope. At the top of the hill was a series of rocks with caves nestled within them. Many of the pedestrians standing around the bus had fixed their gaze on the caves. I assumed that something of interest was up there, so I gazed in that general direction with them.

As we waited, we suddenly heard a roar of cheers and screams arise from the onlooking crowd, and from one of the caves on top of the hill came about a dozen men. At first, it seemed they were all policemen, and they began to march down the hill toward us. Soon, I could see a man who was not uniformed walking in the middle of the mob. It looked as though the police had arrested him. The roar from the crowd continued to grow, and suddenly men ran from the street up toward the police escorting the prisoner. They had machetes in their hands, and they charged the cops with a reckless, thundering yell, and the police scattered in every direction. The arrested man who was left standing, hands cuffed behind his back, looked at the mob racing toward him and simply fell to his knees. He bowed his head, and the first swipe of a machete came down and connected. Blood spurted. The man fell, and the rest of the mob came and finished him off by cutting the alleged criminal into a hundred pieces.

The scene ended with the driver explaining to us that this man was an alleged child rapist who had sexually assaulted one of the girls in his village. He had been hiding in the caves. Though the police declared that, "Justice would be served," the villagers wanted him dead, so they killed him. This was being explained to us as we watched the police return, pick up the various pieces of the man's body, toss them into a body bag, and toss the body bag into the trunk of a patrol car. The police dispersed the crowd, and traffic moved along again.

I did not fully grasp the fact that I had witnessed a murderous capital punishment in a third-world country. First a random man was alive, and then he was dead at the hand of his fellow villagers. How short life seemed to me in that fleeting instant. A few minutes later, we arrived at the infirmary. If I thought witnessing that murder was eye opening, I was in for a real shocker here!

The infirmary consisted of a long, rectangular, open-air corridor filled with beds. The beds were filled with sick or dying people, and the men and women who saw us coming attempted to stand to greet us. There were a few workers who almost demanded that these sick people give us a proper welcome. I felt badly, for most of them looked old and tired. I had no idea what was wrong with them—what illnesses they had or what circumstances had landed them in this place—but my young heart ached for them.

I did not feel comfortable at the infirmary at all, and I was trying to figure out what to do, when, without warning, a woman worker handed me some nail clippers and pushed me gently in the center of my back until I reached the side of a bed. The worker brought a bucket of water, and I proceeded to wash the feet of an elderly man and cut his toenails. It was most unpleasant, but after I had finished, something in me felt good. Contrary to what my mind said I should be feeling—probably nausea accented with the occasional dry heave—I felt a strange sense of satisfaction combined with joy. I cannot put it into words very well, but in the warm smile of this elderly gentleman, who was dying a most unpleasant death, I had gained something unseen—something far more valuable than money. For a moment, I was honestly happy to be in Jamaica, scrubbing the feet of a Jamaican outcast in the blistering heat.

The day ended, and I remember the men and women of our group weeping aloud during our nightly meeting because of the atrocity they had witnessed and the condition of the so-called infirmary, which housed those precious people. Our group was comprised of mostly older men and women, middle-aged to elderly, so Dan and I didn't fit in too well. The nightly meeting was a dramatic scene. It seemed the older our group members were, the more likely they were to outwardly express their emotion. Dan and I simply sat there quietly, pondering the events of the day and watching the emotions of others bubble to the surface.

I really did not know what to think about it all. Watching the murder of that alleged rapist was certainly the most unexpected event of the day, and my mind rested on the thought of how short this life can really be. One moment you're alive, and the next minute you're dead—it can happen that quickly. We never expect it to, but we see it happen to others all the time. I pondered whether or not that man had ever heard about Christ before and if he was a Christian. How many of the murderers were Christians? It got me thinking about our own capital punishment system in the States, and I questioned where the line is that distinguishes punishment from murder. In the case of capital punishment, are they one and the same? Soon, the nightly meeting ended and the group dispersed to their individual rooms.

On another occasion, our little group went to a youth correctional facility where we visited with and encouraged the inmates. It was located deep within a lush forested area. This was a boys' facility housing 150 kids. They were separated from one another based upon age. Once we arrived, the team leader separated us into smaller groups, and I was told to go and hang out with the eighteen-year-olds and lifers. They were either eighteen *or* sentenced to life in prison and were awaiting transport to another jail. I was very intimidated for the first half of our visit. Some of the boys had murdered, many had raped, and some had stolen. I had never been around people like this before, so I was scared to death.

Soon though, as we began to converse, the mood went from scary and intimidating to warm and friendly. We talked about America and Japan, and they asked questions about life outside of Jamaica. We discussed the school systems in other countries, and these kids even ventured into some political questions that I couldn't keep up with. Through talking to these kids, I realized that the only separation that existed between them and me was in my mind. I assumed these kids were different than I, based upon their predilection for unlawful activity, but the only differences between us lay in the value systems we were taught. I held high value on not stealing; these kids held high value on not lying. Maybe they held a high value on avenging the wrong done to their family, so they felt justified in killing the perpetrator, whereas I may hold a high value on defending myself and might feel perfectly justified in killing another human being in self-defense. Both systems have the same result: the death of one individual and his blood soaked on the hands of the one who was justified in killing.

Through talking to those boys, I realized that the barrier I erected in my mind between us only existed as long as I maintained a naïve and limited perspective of life. At the time, that was as far as I could cognitively take this segregation concept on the similarities instead of differences of people. Every people group has its distinguishing facets, and there are tremendous differences between groups when contrasting their value systems of morality, mannerisms, speech, skin tone, preferences, and food. But at the end of the day, people are still people. I have a lot more in common with the inmate in Jamaica than I do with my dog, but I feel utterly comfortable around my dog. This is simply because I'm used to associating with the dog, the dog does not pose a threat to me, and I have relative control over the dog.

As our group assembled and boarded the bus to go back to the guesthouse, I remember thinking, "Man, I could be friends with some of those guys ... they were all right." What a paradigm shift! My perspective was broadened at that very moment, but didn't come into full fruition until years later, when I practiced looking at people in love rather than hate, which is often derived from fear.

Life in Hopewell was interesting. At any given moment, there seemed to be six to twelve young men hanging around outside our compound gate. They minded their own business and did not take too much notice of us. One evening I decided to walk into town to buy a Jamaican patty. (A patty is a local food that consists of soft, warm doughy bread wrapped around meat or cheese ... like a jelly-filled donut. Very tasty.)

After I exited our compound gate, a group of men surrounded me and began to tease and harass me, most of which I could not understand. Suddenly one of them grabbed me and said, "You come to Jamaica? You no leave Jamaica wit'out f---in' a black girl, mon!" He physically turned me to the right and began to walk me to a small hut. He continued with, "It's OK, mon, she's me sista,' and she loves a white boy. I make you a good price for 'er." I began to panic, not knowing if I could escape without being raped! I looked at the guy and said, "No, I'm not here to be with your sister." He took it as a joke and continued to walk me toward the hut, so I stopped walking and repeated myself, and this time he took his hands off me. I walked the other direction, and the men taunted me and called me racist for not wanting sex with the guy's sister.

This type of harassment was commonplace in Hopewell. If a man was not trying to get me to buy the services of a woman in his household, he was trying to sell me ganja for a "good price." It was overwhelming, and I hated exiting the compound. I didn't want to smoke their weed, have sex with their women, or do anything else, but the peddlers were everywhere and unavoidable. I remember thinking, "If America were this poor, we would probably all be doing the same thing as these people because they have no other means of generating income." A man becomes desperate when he feels the pressure to provide for his family, and desperate times call for desperate measures. With the absence of work, why not try to take advantage of the foreigner? I count it a blessing that their morality prevented them from mugging and robbing me. The big eye opener for me was dealing with the desperately poor. I do not believe they meant any offense by trying to sell me one of their services; instead, they were simply doing what they had seen work in the past. As far as they knew, all Westerners love sex and drugs, so that is what they offered me.

Visiting poverty-stricken Jamaica was simply a unique experience I was glad to have. It wasn't until later that it became clear that Jamaica was a training camp for situations I would experience later in life. A few years after graduating high school, I went to Afghanistan as a United States aid worker with a non-governmental organization, and I experienced much of the same hostility I witnessed in Jamaica. I was able to relate better to the average Afghan's perspective of the shortness and futility of life after being in Jamaica. It was easier for me to understand how certain people become outcasts. In poverty-stricken countries such as Jamaica or Afghanistan, an elderly man or woman becomes a burden on the already-struggling family. Outcasts in both countries are so labeled when the sick or elderly person's family is unable to provide for their care. I watched the same violent means of capital punishment get played out in Afghanistan as I did in Jamaica.

I still wonder what it was that actually compelled me to go to Jamaica; I honestly don't know. One thing I do know is that the time I spent there ignited a burning in my heart to be among the chewed-up and spat-out people of the world. I know that my experiences in Jamaica, and later in Afghanistan, had significant influence on the direction of my heart's calling. I love the intensity, high stakes, and heartfelt relationships that I experienced out on the field. And in a way, I feel most alive in that place of high risk. Maybe that is why I didn't want to come back from Jamaica. Returning to Woodland Park felt like being ushered back into a prison cell. But, in what seemed like a blink of an eye, Dan and I were back home enjoying the remainder of our summer vacation.

THE IDENTITY
IMPERATIVE

09

Dan and I returned from our two-week trip to Jamaica just in time for the local Woodland Park Fourth of July celebration of 1994. We saw many of our peers at the festivities, and I found it difficult to express what I had witnessed on our trip. People tend to only be able to conceptualize what they have experienced themselves. Many of our experiences in Jamaica went over their heads. After about a week of telling stories to those who asked, "How was the trip?" only to see their eyes gloss over as they tuned us out, I limited my answers to, "It was fun. Jamaica is hot and beautiful, and the people were great." Jamaica faded into my memory as I started my freshman year.

Because of some success in football the year before, I was recognized as a jock. This peer group of athletes soon became my world. When I was not practicing, I was lifting weights, and when I was not doing that, I was either sleeping or stuck in school. Gradually, the rebellion of my peers became the norm, and I was more comfortable with abusive language, the sex-driven culture, and even some illegal actions. Almost everything we talked about or did revolved around sex, drugs, or profanity. I became more comfortable with the perverse conversations of my friends and more relaxed about my values and standards. I was conforming for the sake of fitting in.

One day after school, I was in the high school weight room. Many of us were committed to lifting weights during the off-season, so there were about a dozen teammates lifting with me. One of the guys who often harassed me and challenged me to fight him in eighth grade was also in the weight room. I do not remember the details, but a conflict arose between us, and in predictable fashion, he challenged me to a fight. I was bench-pressing at the time, being spotted by one of my friends. This guy began to taunt me with verbal challenges of, "Come on, you think you're bad? Bring it outside, and I'll show you how much of a pansy you really are." He went on for about a minute as I debated about shutting this kid up for good. I finished a set and racked the weights. I looked up at my buddy Jamie, and he gave me a look as if to say, "Go kick this kid's a--." And it actually seemed like a really good idea.

I shot a look at the ridiculing boy and told him to lead the way. I followed him to the student parking lot where he turned around, continued to taunt me, and began to take off his shirt. He wouldn't shut up. Some other students came out and stood around, eagerly watching the drama unfold. Most of them were guys on the basketball team, which had just finished practice. My buddy Jamie was held back in the weight room by a coach, who saw what was going on and wanted to ensure the fight wouldn't become unfair for the other guy.

After this little enemy of mine got his personal belongings in order, he walked toward me acting very tough as he kept taunting me. I didn't say much, but as soon as he got close to me, I popped him in the mouth. He staggered back and looked at me in utter disbelief. I'm not sure what he was expecting from this so-called fight. He came toward me again, now yelling, "OK, so that's how it is. You're going to get it now." As his brisk and macho walk brought him back within punching distance, I was surprised to find that he was still looking to engage in a verbal, pushing-and-shoving match. While he was mid-sentence, I sent him another swift punch that connected somewhere on his forehead. He shot me a look as he staggered back, astonished that I was throwing punches without properly going through the preliminary shoves and trash-talking. At that point, he'd had enough of the abuse and charged me, head down and eyes tightly shut. His adrenaline finally kicked in, and the fight became a street brawl.

When the guy walked into school the next day, news of our fight had reached the four corners of the building, and his face was proof of who had won. That fight successfully spiked my popularity and earned me an unhealthy level of respect. I basked in the glory of "one who ought not be messed with" and became more arrogant in my treatment of others.

By the end of my sophomore year, I walked the halls of school with an assurance that I could not be beaten in a fight. I never went into a fight actually feeling fearless, but the mask of fearlessness became my identity. I chose to believe that nothing could or would frighten me in school, though in reality, there were times that I was scared to death! I did not look for trouble, but if trouble came for me, I was confident that I could give it a whooping like it had never felt.

The only trouble that I remember actively looking for was when someone was being bullied by a bigger kid. I had such a hatred of bullies from my time in Japan that I enjoyed searching for the guy in school who was perpetrating this injustice of picking on a smaller person. I'd have a wonderfully good time making the bully feel like a sissy. However, I never considered myself a bully, because I was fighting injustice and bringing what I thought was justice to a defenseless person. Inadvertently, however, I became known as a bully and a jerk—the paramount character of what I hated growing up in Japan.

Around the same time during my freshman year, I experienced my first crush. A good friend of mine had been dating a girl, and because I was friends with him, I got to know her as well. My friend and this girl eventually broke up and stopped hanging out. But because I had gotten to know her, we remained friends. She was involved in sports, and, largely because of my friendship with her, I chose to take part in track and field in the spring of my freshman year. The relationship my friend and this girl had was clearly history, so she and I became closer and did a lot together. She was so great, pretty, kind, accepting, loving ... We did more and more together. Soon, I found that I was falling for this strange and new relationship, which was unlike anything I had ever known.

Things were going along well until one day, when I called her and she sounded strange on the phone. I remember feeling an uneasiness in my stomach after I hung up. A few days later, she told me that she'd been "involved" with someone during that conversation, and that is why she might have sounded preoccupied. I was devastated and felt a lump grow in my throat. She admitted that the other person was none other than my friend, her former boyfriend. For some reason, that news did not phase me as much as her betrayal in inviting another guy to her home for some casual intimacy.

My buddy came up to me at school a day or so later and apologized profusely. I had no problem accepting his apology because he was one of the few people who accepted and showed kindness to me when I first arrived in the eighth grade. But the dramatic loss of an emotional connection with that girl as well as her displayed view of my worth put me into a temporary funk. I was unable to sleep well, eat much, or be happy. I was so sad. The way I handled the news of this betrayal proved to me that the feelings I had for this girl were real.

After that experience, I became a real jerk to the girls in high school. The pain I felt from this first failed relationship combined with my nonexistent relationships with girls in Japan were enough for me to distrust women in general. I treated them like objects rather than people. Their feelings stopped mattering, and their opinions became worthless—I adopted the stereotypical belief that a woman's worth consists of her ability to cook, clean, and be sexy.

By the time I was a senior, I was a full-fledged bully to most guys and an absolute jerk to most females. I always had to be stronger, faster, meaner, and better than the next guy. I gave people more and more flack and belittled them until I saw myself on a pedestal high above my peers. I had many delusions of grandeur, worth, and power.

With all my heart, I believed the lies I told myself, and through the process, any fullness and beauty in the relationships I had with friends and family grew more shallow until I left Woodland Park after graduation as a hard and calloused young man. I intimidated others with fear (because, of course, I was the epitome of fear). If challenged, I never backed down. My mission in life was to punish people for their abusive words by being abusive myself.

I finally got to a point where I couldn't be anything but fearless— or the facade I worked to create would be lost. Old hurts tormented me and kept me from ever showing myself in the accurate light of afraid or hurting. I feared that people might not like me, respect me, or revere me. It was an ugly identity I chose to wear.

Because I didn't need to demand affirmation or respect from parents and authority figures, I was able to continue to work with what was not broken—the mask of competence—in the continued search for affirmation. As I became more violent and abusive toward my peers in school, I made a conscious effort to be respectful and appropriate before parents and those in authority. I discovered that I could maximize affirmation and respect by being two different people for two different groups.

I often took a stand for the abused teacher as students threw things, cussed, and behaved as disrespectful delinquents. I even made a student apologize to a teacher for his disgraceful behavior, threatening to beat him up if he didn't. By behaving in this way—respecting authority figures and simultaneously demanding respect from peers—I was able to feel the satisfaction of being both respected and affirmed.

As my identity as bully, jerk, and jock grew, I found that a sick joy often accompanied the harassment I levied on others. As the cycle mandated that I do more, I lusted after more. By the time I was a senior in high school, I was extremely abusive toward innocent peers in largely the same way that I had been abused as a child by bullies in school. The power that came from handling others was addicting.

This concept of exercising power over others points to the beginning manifestations of the eternal perpetrator. A boy who grows up being physically abused by his father will often manifest similar actions as an adult. I found comfort in knowing that I had gone from victim to perpetrator. Though abusive behaviors were what I hated the most growing up, I had been hurt to a point where the fact that I was now the abuser did not matter. What did matter was that, in my abusive behaviors, I found security in knowing that I was in control.

During high school, I had an avid desire for affirmation, respect, and reverence. What I did not know was that my heart's desire was not to be respected or affirmed as much as it was to be loved. Affirmation and respect were largely indistinguishable from love because of the influence of the appearance of strength in Japanese culture. As I stood in my false identity, I was suppressing the reality of pain and hurt in my past life. Likewise, as I suppressed pain and hurt to a place of nonexistence, I exhibited strength and an ability to conquer in difficult situations. When the lie that I am able to conquer humanly—without any help from my Creator or man—becomes a belief in my life, I am living within the identity of the mask of strength. If I need no help from God or man but choose to believe that I can handle all things on my own, I also have no need for love, because love is found in relationships.

All masks work together quite well, don't they? When the mask of strength became my identity, I discredited my need for love and chose to live as the lord and conquer of my own path. By living within this false reality, the stage was set for the mask of fearlessness and competence to thrive and grow. Respect and affirmation were indistinguishable to me from love because I chose to make the mask of strength my reality. If I could have made the distinction between counterfeit and true respect, I probably would not have chosen the mask of strength, nor identified myself through fearlessness and competence. The mask of fearlessness helped to nurture my need for respect, for I was afraid of not being respected and affirmed. The mask of competence was affirmed through authority figures, and I needed their affirmation more than anything to fill the void I felt in my heart.

I later asked myself, "If pain doesn't exist, and if there is no need for love, and if I am my own lord and conqueror, why do I strive in reckless abandon to be filled with respect and affirmation from others?" Had I stopped to think about where I was and what I was doing in high school, I might have seen all the holes in my pursuit of what I thought was love.

The other mask I wore was that of perfection, which grew into an identity after I had graduated high school. Because of the real pain I endured in Japan of not fitting in with my peers, I believed this mask when it lied to me and told me to place higher value on conforming to the group and lower value on finding out who I was. This mask was effective in telling me, "You're different, so if you try to be you, you will always feel the pain of not being included." I was the stereotypical jock in high school, and my zealous desire to be the poster child of this group was largely due to the lie I believed. The dangerous realities of this mask and the grossness of my rebellion did not begin until I moved away from my family after graduation.

RUNNING

10

FROM GOD

During my junior year, my buddy Jamie and I loaded my parents' minivan with personal belongings and our little brothers, Andy and Ian, and took a road trip to Las Vegas and California over spring break. The primary purpose of the trip was simply to take a "roadie" and exercise our independence. We drove out to California and checked into a small hotel in Anaheim. We ate at restaurants, drove through Compton, had dinner in Chinatown, went to the Shrine, and visited the red carpet as celebrities arrived for the Academy Awards. There was no schedule; we just enjoyed our days as they came.

The trip became very significant to my personal future as we drove away from L.A. and into Las Vegas on our return home. We had a reservation at the Luxor Hotel and two days to spend hanging out in the City of Sin. I had experienced Vegas once during a family vacation, but never to the extent that I did this time. It was because of this trip that I decided to move there after graduation. Deep down, my heart's desire to live in Las Vegas had little to do with the college I attended and everything to do with the lusts of my flesh.

We spent the first day and night in utter amazement at the sheer magnitude of the strip—all the lights, the glitz, the glamour. We hung out at the pool, worked on our tans, and enjoyed the food and atmosphere of Las Vegas. In those first few hours, I felt a sickening pull on my heart toward the lusts of greed, women, money, and power. Everywhere I looked, there were demonstrations of sex, money, and power being shown in the symbols and very life of the city. As the sun went down over the strip, we ventured outside with everyone else and encountered the free pornography distributed by hordes of illegal immigrants. It seemed more limousines existed in Vegas than the population of Woodland Park, and they slowly crept to and from, catering to the wealthy and beautiful people. Everywhere I looked, there seemed to be a scantily clad woman or two on the arm of some guy. I became lost in the desire for the life I was beholding in this beautiful, sick city. Las Vegas did for me what I suspect it does for so many others who visit—it brought to life the fantasies of my deep and dark sinful desires.

Soon after arriving in Las Vegas, I became compulsive about renting a limo and riding around the city. I wanted to feel rich and powerful. There was a distinct pull on my heart to feel what being important was like. As we looked into getting a limo, we became discouraged because they were too expensive for our limited budget. However, I did not give up and eventually found a solution to our dilemma in a small and inconspicuous advertisement in the phone book that said, "Free Limo!" I became excited and said with joy, "Hey, it says here we can get a free limo!" Then, I noticed the small print, and it said, "to Club Exotica from any hotel on the strip." Jamie and I talked about it and decided to go, though we had to leave Andy and Ian back at the hotel. They were both too young to get into the strip club. Something in my gut told me it was a bad idea, but the desire for pleasure and lust was too overbearing for my will, so I picked up the phone and dialed the limo driver.

That night, we dressed in our best and headed down to the lobby of the Luxor Hotel to await our white stretch limo. There were many limos picking up the beautiful people, and finally we spotted ours, as the driver had a sign with my name on it. Jamie and I walked over to the car, strutting with confidence as onlookers watched and must have marveled at these two young men climbing into a limo!

The car crept away, and we were soon lost in the glamour of cruising down Las Vegas Boulevard in a stretch limousine. After creeping up the traffic-laden strip, the driver turned off the glitzy street and onto a very dark alley. A few more turns took us back into a warehouse district where neither Jamie nor I wanted to be.

Up a long, dark alley there was a small sign that read, "Club Exotica," and an arrow pointing to the left. This place was impossible to find, unless you knew where you were going. The darkness of the alley was unlike a normal dark alley at night—it seemed as though there was a cloud that loomed over the region, a cloud that represented despair, hopelessness, and remorse.

Although we were feeling uneasy, we got out of the limo and walked to the front door. The bass from the music inside the club added to my insecurities as the enormous bouncer looked suspiciously at my ID. But the ID verification only lasted a moment. "This way, gentlemen," *he said and ushered us into the club.*

There were naked women everywhere, and it became a sensory overload for me. Part of me was embarrassed to look at the girls, but the other part of me was compelled to gaze and become lost in lustful fantasy. It was as though my heart was pumping not blood but desire through my veins. Jamie had been somewhat reluctant to come to this place, though he wanted the limo ride as much as I did. So when the girls came and offered him a "private dance," he refrained with confidence. I, on the other hand, desperately desired the most intimate experience possible, and I couldn't get enough of the sinful feelings of pleasure that raced through my body at beholding the flesh around me.

Soon, I found a girl to whom I gladly gave my final $20 in exchange for a few minutes of her pleasure. With every point of contact between her body and mine, a vampire of lust bit me; with each rub, caress, whisper, and gesture, she coaxed and led me further into a company of millions of lust-driven people. I can recall the song played, and reality merged with fantasy as truth blurred with untruth.

I now understand the phrase "sold my soul to the devil," for I did just that in exchange for the birth of a war on my heart that will never cease. For $20 and five minutes of pleasure, I had no idea that the remainder of my life would be a battle between the compulsive desires of my flesh and the heart-knowledge I have of truth and righteousness. Have I ever satisfied the desires of my heart? No, but I know beyond a shadow of a doubt that my flesh will always try, until the nature of my inner drive toward lust is replaced with something more powerful.

Until we exited that club at three in the morning, I was
on a utopist cloud. But as soon as Jamie and I stepped
outside, the shame and guilt of sin sank to the depth of my
stomach. I thought I might throw up the beer I was given
at the club. I felt gross and small and evil. We had no
more money for a ride to the Luxor, so Jamie and I walked
many miles back to Las Vegas Boulevard and our hotel. I
felt tired, dirty, and in need of rest as I climbed into bed.
Though the pain of shame was heavy on me, the lust I had
for power, money, and women proved greater. I eventually
made official my decision to move to Las Vegas once I
graduated in search of a life of prosperity.

My senior year may have looked exciting and fun, but on the inside I was exhausted. The respect I had received from people was turning into a subtle disregard for who I was. My friends seemed to be less interested in hanging out with me, and the girls generally disliked who I had become. However, my pride propelled me further and further, to a point that I had no close friends at all. My buddy Dan, with whom I went to Jamaica, began to hang out with a crowd outside of our school that I didn't know, so our paths separated. My buddy Jamie got a girlfriend, so his time was largely spent in his relationship, and we began to walk in different directions, as well. Other than those two guys who had originally accepted me for who I was, I did not feel all that close to anyone. Many of my football buddies were getting into drugs, so our paths gradually drifted apart.

Within my group of athlete friends, the progression of drug use was ironic. I was one of the first jocks to smoke dope during my sophomore year. My insecurities and my need to appear fearless helped me make the choice to try it without much hesitation. Under the stipulation that I was only "dabbling" and "experimenting" in the stuff, I tried pot with a few friends late one night and laughed myself silly, but I recall thinking it was not all that great. When my extended group found out that I had smoked dope, a few of them began to terrorize me about making that choice. I was called "ganja boy," "loser," and "addict"; all the while, I maintained that it was a one-time thing. By the time I was a senior, drugs had become common with nearly every one of those guys who once ridiculed me, but at this point, I was the one condemning that behavior. During my senior year, I found myself distanced from those guys as they elevated drug-use above friendship—that was how I saw it, anyway. But the combination of my insensitivity, condemning attitude, and arrogance toward others was probably much more of the reason I found myself standing emotionally alone as graduation drew nearer.

I knew I wanted to leave the state and attend the University of Nevada, Las Vegas (UNLV), but I also knew that I had no money. My folks suggested that I pray for the funds needed to go and plant myself in Las Vegas, so I did. Praying to God was something that I had abandoned earlier in my high school career, but it seemed as good of an option to generate funds as any other. During the years we lived in America, there were numerous times when my parents found themselves in need of money. Mom and Dad regularly prayed for the funds needed to get through the month, and money never failed to come in. As I found myself short of the money I needed for my move to Vegas, my folks encouraged me to do the same, and sure enough, a check came for me in the mail from a Christian family whom I did not know. The check was written in the amount of $3,000—exactly what I needed to make the transition from Colorado to Nevada. The donors said, "We feel this money should go to your son for his continued educational endeavors."

Before heading to college, Jamie and I went to Australia to play football with an all-state team from Colorado. During the trip, I had a chance to reflect on high school and my life in America. As I looked back, there were memories I was proud to talk about and memories that I was not proud of at all. However, I felt that I had done a pretty good job of sticking to my core values of morality. I graduated high school a virgin and had not engaged in much sexually promiscuous behavior. Not to say I didn't have opportunities to break the vow I made to remain sexually pure, but I was on a string of good decision-making in that arena. I had tried drugs, but had no desire to make them a part of my life. I did not smoke, and I hardly drank. I had succeeded in sports, and my grades warranted admission to college. Overall, I remember being quite satisfied with my performance in high school ... except for the nagging emptiness in my heart.

One morning as I walked alone on the beach of the Gold Coast, I felt a pain emerge in my heart due to the poor quality of my relationships in high school. My relationships with both guys and girls were very shallow. I had lost most of the friendships that used to be close; I was distanced from my folks emotionally; and God was a moot point. I debated what I should do to try to mend some of the broken relationships, but my pride won out. My record in high school was pretty good, outside of relationships, so I pushed the hurt away, in classic form, and returned to America optimistic about moving on and disallowing pain to become a stumbling block.

A week after I returned from Australia, my family drove me out to Las Vegas for my proclaimed purpose of going to school. The transition was difficult. We arrived in Vegas and stayed at the Luxor Hotel once again. The first few days were spent taking care of orientation stuff at UNLV and getting to know the campus. I purchased a motorcycle for $2,200. A contact of mine called in a favor to a friend who owned a small, rundown apartment complex just north of the strip on Charleston and Main Street. The owner let me stay there for close to two months for only $550. The school semester would begin in seven weeks, and then I would move into the UNLV freshman dormitory. I believed that my $3,000 budget would be sufficient, regardless of my employment situation.

My family only spent a week in Vegas with me. As the day of their departure drew nearer, stress mounted. It must have been tough on my folks, for I doubt they knew why I was so neurotic about getting out of Woodland Park—I didn't even know. My family supported me as best as they could, though I was becoming more emotionally shut off from everything around me. Finally, the day came when I said goodbye to my family, and my heart ached. A nasty little emotional trap called pride inhibited me from telling them how much I loved them and how much I would miss them. I felt I had to stand emotionless and strong so they could drive away knowing that I would be OK. I showed outward confidence as they loaded up their vehicle and drove off under the hot desert sun.

Suddenly it was quiet. I looked around, and I felt utterly alone. Tears came to my eyes, and I cried for what seemed like hours in my small, musky room. No matter how much I tried, I could not stop feeling completely alone. Slowly, hours of quietness became days of loneliness, which became weeks of solitude, which birthed depression. I called home a few times, but for the most part I chose not to allow such a show of weakness. Though I wanted to talk to my family, I chose the utter darkness of loneliness, pretending that life didn't hurt as badly as it did.

My average day consisted of waking up, watching TV all day, going for an occasional walk, coming back to the apartment, eating a little something for dinner, and going to bed. I did not talk much during those two months because I had no one to talk to. I was expecting to get a job at a local hotel. Though I called every few days to check up on where they were at in the hiring process, I inevitably got the runaround and was left wondering if I would ever start work.

One morning I woke up, turned on my TV, and found an alarming story on the news as I flipped through the channels. A local news station was airing a live shot from a helicopter of an apartment complex on Charleston and Main Street, the major intersection near my apartment. As I looked at the TV, I soon realized that my apartment complex was being shown on the screen. The news reporter said, "All persons living in or around this vicinity should remain indoors and away from windows. The fugitives are suspected to be hiding out in this area, and police are currently on the search." Just then, I looked outside and noticed a few policemen walking by my window with guns drawn. I decided it was a good day to stay inside. The situation was resolved a few hours later, but I was quite scared.

During my stay in that apartment, I spent a lot of time crying in my bed. I was hurt and sad, and I wondered how to get rid of the pain in my heart. Anytime I talked to someone from back home, I tried to be outwardly confident—that was all I knew how to do. The inner pain I felt remained a secret. I had long ago made a choice not to be hurt by embarrassment or ridicule. I was determined to go forward, but during the first few weeks of my stay in Vegas, I experienced a real-life emotional breakdown.

After weeks of lamenting the sufferings of my life while looking through the lens of my horribly distorted pain perspective, I made a choice that took me down a path unlike any I had ever walked. The path led me into the heart of rebellion and sin, as I literally sold any remainder of my soul to Satan himself. In a fretful combination of hurt, confusion, desire, and determination, I walked out of my little room one evening and headed for a corner market. I arrived at the little store, counted my pennies, and chose to buy a package of cigarettes. I walked away from that shop with a box of Marlboro Reds and went up onto the third-story balcony of the apartment complex. There, looking over the desert landscape as the sun dipped beneath the hills on the horizon, I lit a cigarette as the lights of the city began to pop on.

The twinkle of the Plaza Hotel shined, the neon of the "Adult Superstore" next door flashed, and I found the resolve to walk in a new direction. Before I knew it, I had finished one cigarette and promptly lit another. After a drag, I said aloud, "God, I'm through with You." No sooner did I say those words than a tear came to my eye. I had no idea why, but I felt a deep sorrow in my heart. After another drag, I continued with strength, "I want You to go and never come back to me. You have brought me a life of pain and hurt, and I have absolutely nothing but torment in my heart to show for it. I will create my world by me and for me, and I do not need Your help anymore. With a God like you, what's the use of the devil? So go away and never return." Those were the last words I said to God until 2001; it was 1998 at the time.

God was to blame—that was all I could see through the skewed view I had of my past. Everything was blurry as I peered through the lens of pain, but if I could see anything clearly, it was that God had become my nemesis. God was supposed to be a God of love, but He obviously didn't love me. My course was set, and if I ever hoped to have a life of pleasure, I must delete God from my life . I remember marveling at how hard I cried while giving God a directive to go away from me. With blurred vision, I watched the sun sink over the Las Vegas valley, and the night of mystic wonder began ... but this night would not end for years to come.

With this decision came new resolve, and my life instantly got better, or so was my perception. I left the apartment much more often in search of the world I had decided to build. I did not dwell on the past any longer, but I looked to the future for comfort. I got to know some of the local homeless guys, who introduced me to the infamous "$1 breakfast" at the El Cortez, a steal for anyone on a tight budget. Though I never became friends with those homeless guys, I did enjoy their company. They had a freedom that I longed for. If I felt lonely or sorry for myself, instead of dwelling on it, I made active choices to go and be more a part of society. No longer was I content to sit and be sad in my room. With that exclamation to God, I had found a new and promising resolve to go and recklessly take the desires of my heart!

Mom returned to Las Vegas to help me move into the dormitory at UNLV. It was so great to see her. I remember wishing that Dad and Andy could have come out as well, but having Mom around was a real blessing, both emotionally and physically, as I tackled one of many moves.

Just prior to moving into the dorm room, my job began at the Imperial Palace Hotel, and I took my post at the front desk. The job proved to be a great introduction to work and life in Vegas, and I quickly learned the many facets of my new job.

The pace of life really picked up after I rejected the Lord. Although I didn't notice it at the time, it was as though I blinked, and everything I wanted and desired was suddenly in my lap! No longer did I stress about whether or not I had enough money, because the job finally started. No longer did I stress about having food, because I was finally in the dorm and on the UNLV meal plan. I suddenly had little to worry about, and soon I made a slew of new friends. Life went from horrible and hopeless to exciting and promising with one small rebuke of the One who created me.

During my first semester, I had an ambitious desire to make some serious money and focused primarily on that task. I worked thirty-five to forty hours per week. I also had fun hanging out with some of my new friends in the dorm, and my roommate and I started drinking quite a bit, as he had a solid fake ID. Our room was never without a good stock of Budweiser, so it became a common hangout for the others on our floor that first semester. I had a lot of fun getting to know those who chose UNLV as an institute worthy of their higher scholastic goals ... and for the first time in years, I felt continuous joy in my life as I lived in pursuit of pleasure.

FEEDING
MY FLESH

11

Paradoxically, as soon as I told God to leave me alone, my life improved so much that I became completely distracted from how badly I felt about who I had become and how my past had hurt me. In the absence of God, there seemed to be nothing keeping me from going after all the pleasures that this world had to offer. Slowly, I began to compromise all the values I was brought up to respect. With each compromise, I became more obsessed with finding a cure for the pain in my heart that resulted from compromising the value itself. This led to a snowball effect of more and more sin.

It was difficult to articulate my feelings back then. The reality was that I had bandaged hurts of the past and tried to numb them. However, if someone had asked me how I felt about life, I would have most assuredly said, "Fine," and meant it. The rapidness of life kept me too busy to dwell on my emotional and spiritual needs, but their existence was found in my gluttony and lust.

89

Many times, people would tell me to, "Stop and smell the roses," because it was evident that I was moving at an inhuman pace. This catch phrase speaks to our need as humans to slow down and take a good hard look at who we are as individuals in the context of our surroundings. Doing so was difficult for me because, if done correctly, I knew it would bring painful conviction about the sinful nature of my lifestyle. I knew that if I were to be completely honest with myself, "Fine," was the most blatant of lies. With my full-speed-ahead approach to daily living, it was impossible to stop long enough to realize my own depravity. My personal rebellion kicked into full gear as I walked away from God.

One reluctant compromise led to another, and soon I became so wrapped up in the culture of Las Vegas that I found myself trapped in a whirlpool of sin. The first major value I compromised was sexual purity. My sexual intimacy routine with girls in high school had always been a pathetic moral cop-out—I was never the one who stopped the intimacy, but I did everything in my power to make sure the girl stopped the action for us. I was scared to death of having sex before marriage, which I had always held as a sacred value. I whispered to her every possible reason I could think of not to go all the way. In high school, I was 100 percent successful utilizing this tactic. The reason I preferred to let the girl stop the action was so that I had an alibi when my peers interrogated me about why the sexual episode failed to go all the way. Simply stated, it was much easier to say, "Because she didn't want to, and I'm a gentleman," than to tell the truth, "Because I got scared and chose not to."

In any event, I had no conscious desire to compromise my morals, but I soon realized that the tactic I used in high school would never work in the college setting. I met this particular girl one Friday night. After work the next day, I came back to the dorm; the entire floor was drinking the night away in jubilee, and she was there. Eventually, everyone left for the infamous strip and the party scene that never ends. They asked if I wanted to go, and I said, "No,

I'm tired, I'm just going to go to bed." Everyone left, except the girl, and we ended up talking. Soon, talking led to drunken kissing, and kissing led to drunken sex. I tried to get her to stop the action—my usual tactic—but this time it didn't work. The next morning, this girl was in and out of my life. There is no way I could pick her out of a lineup today, and my heart still hurts for that compromise.

I woke up the next day feeling conflicting emotions. I felt remorse for what I had compromised. I felt nervous and immoral for committing what I knew spiritually was wrong. But in the absence of God, pleasure seemed so right, and the emotional connection seemed significant enough to be truth. I also felt relief. In high school, sex was a fearful thing to me; it caused me to question my own sexual orientation. I sometimes heard a voice tell me, "You must be gay if you don't want this." After my first sexual encounter, I could say with confidence, "No, I'm not gay because I do want this."

However, my conflicting feelings made me extremely confused. Nothing in my life was a steadfast conviction anymore. When I started compromising the values that I thought were important, I got caught in a vicious cycle of trying to legitimize the sinful actions so I wouldn't feel so badly about what I had done. On one hand, I knew that it was wrong because of the shame, guilt, or conviction I felt deep within my heart. But on the other hand, I was too scared to stop and deal with my inner hurts and uncover the pain of my past. I believed the only relief I could attain was to fill the lusts of my heart with sinful pleasure.

Over the next few months and years, I had numerous sexual partners. With each episode of sexual intimacy, the positive feelings diminished and the negative feelings became more distinguishable. As remorse grew on my conscience, I numbed the bad feelings with my need to connect. I began an endless search for the affections of others through sexual intimacy, but each sexual encounter gave less emotional relief and more spiritual anguish. In my mind, I debated:

Can the feeling of real connection once again be attained?
Why do I feel so sick inside, as if my life is all wrong?
Because that girl last night was a real nut case and didn't have it together.
Why do the freaky-weird girls cling to me?
I'm strong, and I'm fearless ... girls like that because they are not.
How I desire to have a relationship though ...
But what girl in this day and age will have a relationship outside of sex?
This is true, what girl would?
Certainly not the girls I like.

I had hundreds of these internal debates. Had I stopped to consider them, I might have realized that the very nature of the debate was cause for concern. But I didn't, because life was flying by way too fast, and the noise and distractions of this world continued to lure me further into the abyss of rebellion.

My first semester at UNLV ended on what seemed like a real high. I was excited about the emotional connection I was feeling toward one of the girls in my life, and I had made some good friends in the dorms. As everyone left for Christmas break, I was one of two in my group who decided to remain in Vegas. We moved into a Budget Suites and enjoyed the warm winter in the Vegas valley. I was moving ninety miles an hour when my family came out to visit me over Christmas. We had a good time, and I continued to focus on work and personal advancement as my ambition to become wealthy and powerful burned within me.

The second semester of school started on a negative note. Soon after classes began, the girl whom I really liked started to act strange and was caught having sex with her ex-boyfriend. She was then kind enough to inform me that I was an item she used to spark jealousy in her ex. It crushed me, but I was ready, willing, and able to simply delete her from my life and treat her as badly as she had treated me. This breakup created an atmosphere of strife and disconnect on our dorm floor that used to do just about everything together. My roommate dropped out of college after that first semester due to a gambling problem and a sudden lack of funds. He was a really big part of my social circle at UNLV, and I missed him dearly. A few of the others in our group dropped out, as well. The dropouts were replaced with different students, but the atmosphere in our dorm simply couldn't be replaced. I distanced myself from the girl I had once liked, consequently distancing myself from other mutual friends.

A guy named Joe became my new roommate. He was a nice guy, but somewhat strange. He was disrespectful to women and seemed to be intimidated by other guys. The others on my floor seemed a bit cautious around Joe and never really embraced him as one of the group. No one knew what it was, but there was simply something about him that didn't settle well with us.

One day, I returned to my dorm room to write a paper for class using Joe's computer. I was shocked to find pictures of male child pornography littering the screen. I was taken aback, but Joe and his oddities became clearer to me. I cleared the screen and typed my paper. I kept the knowledge to myself until some time later, when Joe and I were up late talking, and I asked him about his life.

The conversation I had with Joe took a course of its own. As I confronted Joe, my heart's desire was not to belittle him or put him down, but rather to try to understand what he went through that could possibly lead him to a place of finding joy in child pornography. The spiritual bondage that Joe was under soon became quite evident to me, and a truth about the nature of God was revealed to me through my interactions with Joe. The conversation went something like this:

"Joe," I began, "I'm not sure how to bring this issue up, so I'm simply going to ask you."

"What is it?" he said.

"I got onto the computer the other day and noticed a picture that really freaked me out. Do you know what I'm talking about?"

He paused, and said, "Yes, I do." Then, suddenly he exclaimed, "And what is it to you, anyway?"

"Well, nothing really," I said, a bit surprised with his stern retort, "but looking at pictures of little boys doing older men seems a bit strange and wrong, wouldn't you agree?"

"Well ... what can I say," he began to calm down. I was expecting him to say something else, but no other words came. I wondered if I should take the conversation any further, and suddenly found myself asking him, "Joe, why don't you tell me about your past."

Joe went on to tell me of a tree fort he had built with some friends while growing up in Reno, Nevada. He said that he always got along with the older kids in his neighborhood, and the boys who built the tree house with him were all a bit older than he was. They were good friends of his, and Joe told me how alive he felt when hanging out with them. Then he said, "One day we were in the tree fort together, and one of the boys told me to take my shorts and underwear off. He told me that he could make me feel good. I told him, 'No, I don't need to feel good.' But the boy insisted and told me that all of the high school kids were doing it and that I should also do it if I wanted to be a part of their group."

Joe paused for a moment, then continued. My stomach began to curl as he told me the details about the first sexual experience he ever had. Joe said, "From that moment, I have never been able to look at younger boys without everything else going black. It is like my eyes will see a young boy, and I can't help but look at him as though I'm looking through a dark tunnel. All I can feel and think about is ..." The conversation faded into silence, and I remember feeling hurt for Joe.

Next, without any notice, I began to speak in a way I had never talked to anyone before. I said, "Joe, you have gone to psychiatrists, and you have undergone therapy, but nothing has ever solved this problem of yours, am I right?" I shocked myself with this comment, because Joe had not talked about how he had ever attempted to combat his issues.

"Well, yes, you are right," he said with surprise.

"This is because you seek for the help you need in all the wrong places. I know what it is that torments you, and you have a right to know as well."

"OK," Joe said, "what is it?"

"Satan speaks lies, and you listen," I said, without as much as a hint of doubt.

"Oh come on, that's ridiculous," he fired back.

"Would you like me to prove it to you?" I asked, with an unusual amount of gentleness in my voice.

"You can't prove that type of thing, so don't even try."

Then, with an elevated tone I said, "Well, it's absolutely inhumane to dream of sexual encounters with boys who are defenseless. The little children! You yourself are a victim and the very thought of ..."

"Well, what's the matter with it?" Joe screamed as he interrupted me. "So what if I look upon the young meat. Who should really care? After all, I'm only looking at them and dreaming about it, and it's not like I've actually done anything! Besides, these ..."

"Joe," I said with an elevated and authoritative voice, "I call you back in the name of Jesus."

He suddenly stopped short of his rationalizing and looked blankly at me for a moment. A strange calm seemed to permeate the room. I didn't have to say anything else, and soon Joe began to cry. Through bitter tears, he asked the questions that led him to the truth of understanding. "Who was that? Who would say such words and try to legitimize this evil?

You're right, therapy is not what I need. I need this demon of lust to be banished from my life. Can you help me?"

I thought about it for a minute, and told him, "Joe, I don't know that I can help you, but I can probably put you in touch with someone who can. Let's just sleep on it, and you can ask again tomorrow if you're serious."

As I lay in bed, I was overwhelmed and remember feeling like my heart was beating a thousand beats per second. Not just because of the graphically explicit past Joe had only moments before told me about, but also because I, too, did not fully know what had just happened. Somehow, I had asked Joe if he wanted me to prove to him that this problem was not of his own personal psyche. The next thing I knew, I was verbally provoking him to a point that led to the demonic spirit speaking on his behalf, within Joe's own hearing! I knew it was a demonic spirit. Joe himself was suddenly perceptively strong and powerful as he snapped angrily at me when I condemned the action of child molestation. Joe, by nature, was a very soft and gentle guy, who seemed to be somewhat scared of other men his age most of the time. But as he retorted against my convicting words, there was an air of power and authority about him that I had never felt before.

The next day, Joe asked again for help, and I told him about my parents and the ministry that they were led into some years earlier. I told him about deliverance and tried to impart my limited understanding of it.

Interestingly enough, Joe asked to speak to my folks by phone, so I set up the conversation. A few talks later, it was evident to everyone on my dormitory floor that Joe was a changed person—not in charisma or behavior toward his peers, but in a calm and peaceful way. There was no longer a foreboding barrier erected between him and the other female peers, nor was there a weakling

crybaby demeanor about him in the midst of the male peers. It
was also evident that others felt more at ease around him and were
much more receptive to Joe. There was no longer a strong edge
to his persona, and he was invited to hang out with the rest of the
group.

For about two months after the prayer session with my parents
on the phone, Joe experienced a strange and profound joy and
peace that he had not felt in years. His behavior, speech, attitude,
and overall demeanor in front of others, as well as his peers'
sudden acceptance of him, seemed to confirm the positive changes
he was expressing to me.

Then Joe regressed, and I caught him looking at some pictures
on the Internet. I confronted him, and he fell back into the old
routine of legitimizing his actions. He knew he was losing the
joy and peace he had in his heart, so he took steps to try to help
himself. The first step was disconnecting AOL and Internet service
from his computer. However, being a technically savvy guy, Joe
found a way to bypass that control measure and all others he chose
to enact. His final and most desperate attempt to walk away from
the perversion on his heart was his choice to simply fight his urges,
but that lasted only a few days.

As Joe reverted back to his old habits, our peers again began
shunning him, and I had no idea what was going on spiritually. It
seemed contradictory to God's nature to free him only to allow
him back under the bondage. But then again, God made no sense
to me during those years, so I was content to tell Joe, "I don't know,
buddy," when he came and asked me for help. Joe went home for
summer break, and the last time I saw him was on the local news.
The broadcaster said that Joe had been charged with the sexual
assault of two young boys. He received a sentence of about twenty
years and continues to serve it.

After finishing that first year of school at UNLV, I once again
felt largely alienated from my peers and chose to get out of the
dorms as fast as possible. I found a small, one-bedroom apartment

on Pecos Street. I was excited about living alone. Dorm life was full of excessive noise and chaos. It simply was not conducive to my needs during that season, when work and professional advancement meant so much to me.

That summer, I ambitiously sought new employment. The front-desk job I had my first year in Vegas was good, but I knew I could do better. I worked at a very old hotel on the Las Vegas strip, and we catered to high-end sports gamblers as we had a unique sports book. But I desired wealth and power, and I realized that was not attainable from the front desk of this rundown hotel. I was excited to read in the paper that a brand new hotel was hiring for all positions. The hotel was set to open a few months later, but they were hiring now, so I quickly applied. A few weeks later, I was hired to work at this new luxury hotel in a very prestigious position—the hotel management believed that my Japanese capabilities would be a huge asset. I have decided not to disclose the name of this hotel, but will refer to it as the Palace Court Hotel instead.

Weeks before the Palace Court opened its doors to the general public, I found myself in orientation. The Palace Court employed some five thousand people on the day of its grand opening, and excitement among the new recruits was high. I had been hired to work in a department that existed to meet the needs of the Palace Court's guests. Guests would be referred to my department in the event that they were unable to find what they were looking for. I had no idea what all this entailed, but I eagerly desired to learn about and grow in the business of meeting the needs of others.

Suddenly, the Palace Court's grand opening came, and business kicked into full gear. During the grand opening weekend, we housed a number of high-profile people, including executives of our umbrella company, political leaders, and many celebrities. I was in awe of the wealth that surrounded me! We had Ferraris and Lamborghinis parked in our front drive and gorgeous models serving the guests, and I found myself talking to wealthy individuals about their various needs and how the Palace Court might service those requests.

In what seemed like a moment in time, I went from the monotony of checking people in and out at the front desk of a dump to the luxury of catering to the world's elite. The management made it clear that we were not to show partiality to guests based on income. However, they also made it known that we were to fully adhere to the demands and wishes of a confirmed "whale" (a Vegas term used for extremely wealthy individuals). If we ever had a question about it, we had the option of calling a casino executive for inside information on the individual's gaming habits.

The special needs of our clients ranged from honeymoon room decorations to sold-out show or event admission to restaurant reservations to assistance finding drugs or prostitutes. The department I worked in, to its credit, did a relatively good job of adhering to the ethical parameters of the law, and sometimes we chose not to service high-risk requests. But in Vegas, money talks, and we all know what walks, so the way we handled sensitive requests had a lot to do with the green that our clients were willing to put up as collateral.

One day, I was at my small apartment on my day off, taking in the sun at the swimming pool. I remember being consumed with doing my job well, and on this particular day, I felt a little uneasy about how a ticket order had been processed. When guests asked us for tickets, it usually meant that the event was sold out. If tickets are sold out, they can only be purchased through a ticket broker. Ticket brokers walk a very fine line between legal and illegal, as well as ethical and completely immoral. The broker business in Vegas remains a shady business, by all accounts.

As I walked from the pool back to my apartment, I decided that it was worth my concern to give a quick confirmation call to the ticket broker about this order that had unnerved me. The person I spoke to happened to be the owner of the business. The individual sounded stressed out, so I calmly asked the person how my order was coming along. This person screamed at me, "I'm not a da-- box office. I'm a ticket broker! I'll call you when I get the thing finished!" With that, I hung up.

A minute later, I called back, and the same individual answered, this time, sounding much calmer. The person said, "I'm sorry, I guess we got disconnected somehow." I was livid, and I retorted with a calm arrogance, "No, we did not get disconnected at all. Actually, I simply hung up on you because I'll have you know right now, I do not tolerate being screamed at, especially by someone I have hired for service. Do you understand me?" There was an awkward silence on the phone and a very brief, "Yes, I will call you when your order is complete," and we hung up cordially.

The next day I walked into work and had a head-on collision with my irate boss. My boss had spent an hour listening to that ticket broker rant and rave about the need to fire me, and he had suffered enough verbal abuse that he was willing to. My boss took me aside and unloaded angrily on me. I was in trouble for hanging up on that particular broker, and I was given a verbal warning not to ever treat this individual this way again. My boss did a really good job of controlling his displeasure, but I could see that I had overstepped my bounds. I took my lashing and left his office in a quiet rage. I vowed in my heart to financially break that particular ticket broker business, no matter how long it took. For the sake of further reference, I will refer to this ticket broker agency as "Broker A."

I did not know how to accomplish my revenge, but I began to look into methods of channeling financial funds away from Broker A and toward a competitor ticket broker, whom we were corporately not supposed to use. The competitor ticket broker agency will be further referred to as "Broker B." Because we had been directed not to use Broker B as a first option in the servicing of our guests, the entire operation had to be masked. Together with three other individuals, I worked on a money scam that ended up channeling thousands of dollars away from Broker A and into the hands of Broker B.

The slow demise of Broker A became my personal joy. Together with my fellow cohorts, who also despised the business methods of Broker A, we saw our pockets get filled with illegitimate moneys at the expense of the person who had screamed at the wrong man. I felt unstoppable. I remember preaching the phrase, "Keep your friends close, but your enemies closer," as I attended the little functions of Broker A, purposefully maintaining casual friendship with the person I despised. As time passed, Broker A fell deeper and deeper into financial turmoil, and I maintained a poker-faced, outwardly calm manner, while internally mocking the dim-witted person.

I continued to sink deeper into the pit of rebellion. I found myself attending prizefights, mingling at exclusive parties, eating expensive food, basking at the spas, and playing a whole lot of golf—all of which are acceptable things to do, but their sinful illegitimacy came from my heart's position about my involvement. I lost touch with most of my peers from UNLV as my world became the men and women with whom I worked and serviced. I was by far the youngest in the group, and many of my fellow workers at the Palace Court were established and quite wealthy. They took me to their parties and events, and I shook hands with celebrities from Hollywood, the world of professional sports, and political leaders.

Had I stopped for a moment, I would have seen myself living the very life I thought I had always wanted. It came at the expense of compromising anything ethical, but the life itself was one of abundance. At work, there was nothing I would not do for a dollar. If a person walked up to me and asked, "How do I get a woman in this town?" I said, "It remains very dangerous for me to help service this particular request of yours. The benefit has to outweigh the risk, if you know what I mean." Nine times out of ten, the individual would not come back at me with words, but with a Vegas handshake, slipping me a special gratuity for more information. I would then get him in touch with a pimp who had a prostitute available and on call.

During this season of my life, the mask of perfection set in hard. I developed a reputation among those I kept in touch with from high school that was very misleading. Though my lifestyle depicted me as wealthy, I was living paycheck to paycheck, and my bills were always a major stressor. People came to visit me, hoping to experience all the luxury they had heard I was living in. Most of these people were broke college kids who could not afford the lifestyle of luxury, but I was supposedly wealthy enough to give others a glimpse of it—and I kept up the charade.

Around my college friends, I felt that I had to act a certain way. Around my wealthy friends, I felt that I had to act a certain way. Around my parents, I felt that I had to act a certain way. All in all, the fear of failure crippled my ability to admit that I could not keep up. The truth is, for a college kid, I was making a ton of money, but not enough to measure up to the reputation I was creating for myself, under all the other masks of strength, power, and competence. Dan and Jamie were the only two who saw through the masks.

Before I turned twenty-one, I had been served alcohol at numerous high-end functions. As a joke, those who invited me to these events often told bartenders and wait staff that I was too young to drink, and then would demand a drink be brought to the table and set before me. One such time, I was eating dinner with a few friends at a steak restaurant on the strip. We had ordered two bottles of Rothschild Merlot during dinner, and one guy in our party decided to fire up a Cuban cigar as we concluded our meal. We went to the bar, and the bartender said, "You know that Cuban is illegal, right?" One of my friends placed his hand on my shoulder and said, "That's not the only thing illegal in this bar right now. Why don't you give him a glass of Luis-tre" (at $125 per shot). The bartender looked at him, smiled, and said, "Yes, sir."

My twenty-first birthday was spent sitting in a VIP section, along with my brother, Jamie, another friend named Mark, and his wife, at the Staples Center in L.A. watching the Lakers play. We had expensive suits on, and I remember thinking, "My twenty-first birthday is only the beginning of my rise!" I felt in my heart that nothing could slow my momentum. After the game, my group got into a fight with four other preps sitting in the row above us. Jamie started the fight because a drunken member of their group accidentally dumped beer down his back while cheering on a Kobe Bryant fast-break. We walked out of the tunnel, and all hell broke loose as a four-on-four brawl opened up. Hundreds of people watched as I successfully landed a great left-hook that knocked my opponent out. It was the first time I had ever actually KO'd someone. We ran away from Staples Center security and ended up in our downtown hotel, sipping on cocktails and joking that Jamie's fight turned out to be the best birthday gift I could have received— a knockout.

Upon returning to Vegas, I was handed a bottle of Dom Perignon and escorted by my colleagues to Olympic Gardens for a night of "adult play," as the endless birthday continued. One guy in our group spent more than $800 on me and lined up one girl after another for my pleasure. This was truly a life that appeared to be totally fulfilling, but on the inside, I continued to scream for nourishment.

My twenty-second birthday was spent at Picasso, a restaurant in the Bellagio Hotel, with my brother Andy and two friends who decided to treat us to a nice dinner. The final bill for the four of us that night was more than $3,800. The food was good, but I was lost in a daze, and money seemed to have no value to me. I spent it like water, trying to keep up with the lifestyles of my friends, and I refused to admit that I was falling deeper into debt.

As I entered into my twenty-second year of life, burnout was fast approaching. I had experienced so much pleasure while working at the Palace Court for the past two years that fulfilling my lusts was becoming harder to achieve. I was running out of options. I had eaten the finest food, been with the finest women, made plenty of money, met just about everyone I ever wanted—yet as my life slowed down, I realized that pain continued to exist in my heart! Desperation pervaded as I slowly came to understand that I could not sustain this crazy pace. But if my life slowed down, I would not be able to feed my need for pleasure, which meant that I was going to have to deal with my pain. Then one day I was forced to stop and smell the stench of my life, and that season became one of the most painful ever.

EMERGING TRUTHS

12

In early November 2000, my life was moving full-speed ahead. My rebellions in sexual lust, financial scandal, spiritual disassociation from God, devaluation of people, excessive drinking, mammoth pride and arrogance all created a temporal, seemingly secure world. The need for relationships and authentic heart-level connection with people had been replaced with intimate objects: women, toys, and money. It was a horribly stressful time, and then suddenly, one event transformed my world entirely.

My departmental phone rang at the Palace Court one evening, and I saw "Security Main" written on the caller ID. I picked it up, and an officer said, "We need you up in suite 895 immediately." I told him I would be right there and proceeded to the elevators. On my way, I recalled the many other instances when the Palace Court security department had phoned for my help. It always had to do with a Japanese-related security issue. I had assisted in everything from burglary cases to full-fledged manslaughter involving our

Japanese clientele. I wondered what was going on this time as I fixed the collar of my suit in the elevator mirror.

As I walked down the long hallway toward room 895, I noticed a few security guards standing outside. I exchanged pleasantries with them and walked in. A Japanese woman was pacing back and forth; a real intensity was in the room. A few men in suits and the chief of security stood around talking quietly. I asked, "What's going on?" The security chief and another man walked me out of the room and proceeded to tell me that this woman had just alleged that an employee of another hotel had raped her. The hotel where the alleged infraction took place was a sister property of the Palace Court. Because I worked at the Palace Court, the management decided to transfer her to this hotel so that I could care for her.

I walked into the room again and spoke softly with the woman, as she spoke no English at all. She asked, "Did they tell you what happened?" I said, "Yes," and our conversation remained brief. One of the men said, "Why don't you let her know that you are available to her if she needs anything and give her your direct extension. We'll comp whatever she needs, and you can call me if you need to run anything by me. We'll need to meet with her in a few hours, so ask her not to go anywhere unless she first phones you." I relayed the message to the woman, and she agreed, though she was obviously bemused and perplexed.

A few hours later, we were back in the woman's room, and this time only two upper-level managers and the chief of security were with me. They handed me a souvenir bag full of Palace Court goodies and told me to translate, "Tell her, as a gesture of our sorrow for what happened to her, we would like to offer her this gift." The woman looked at me blankly. Then they handed me a check and said, "We would also like to give her this token and buy her flight home to Japan." I translated that statement as she looked at the $5,000 check. Then, the managers handed me a piece of paper, which resembled a small contract. There was a place for the woman to sign at the bottom of the page. The manager explained,

"This is an agreement we would ask her to sign that waives her right to speak of this incident and asks her not to return to Las Vegas again, in exchange for the said settlement of $5,000."

I looked at the agreement and felt emotion bubble up my throat like it had not done in many years. I remembered Jamaica, and the hurt and pain I saw in the eyes of the men and woman in the infirmary who had been chewed up and spat out by society. I saw a man getting murdered without a fair trial. I looked at this woman, and I saw my own daughter—crying, hurt, scared, confused. I did something that very moment that changed the course of my life.

I looked at the woman and said to her in Japanese, "Woman, this is an agreement that states you will not be allowed to speak of this incident ever again. It also says you may never return to Las Vegas. You agree to take the money offered to you, and the hotel receives the assurance that you will not disclose what happened to you, ever." I continued with, "However, woman, you might accurately see that this is not justice. If you see that what they are asking of you is wrong, I invite you to step back, shake your head 'no' to the men, and sit on the couch. You can trust me to handle the rest, and I will promise to fight this for you, but you must trust me."

She thought about it and took a half step backward. She began to shake her head "no" to the men standing in the room, and I watched. One of the men said to me, "No, she's saying 'no,' but try to make her understand that this would be in her best interest. Go, tell her now!"

I looked at the woman, and I said, "Can I get you any food from room service? Maybe some tea or coffee?"

She smiled and said, "Maybe some tea would be nice."

I then said to her, "They are asking me to talk you into signing this piece of paper, but they don't understand Japanese, so I will continue to play this game until they leave, and then I will get you some tea." Her smile enlarged, and a tension left the room.

I looked at the managers and said, "She is not going to sign this agreement, and she does not believe this is in her best interest.

Would you sign it?" They eventually left the room saying, "Try to make her understand; we'll take the news to our superiors."

The news of what was happening with this woman—the way our hotel chain was trying to cover up the incident and the recent development of her refusing to sign the agreement— became everyone's favorite drama within Palace Court middle-management over the next few days. There were rumors, questions, and unofficial warnings to me not to get involved in this situation beyond what was asked of me. I remember feeling unsurpassed power during this rape fiasco. I had the authorization to instigate a multimillion-dollar lawsuit, and why not? Justice, for God's sake, was not being served if a man is allowed to walk up to a single woman's room, open her door, rape her, and then get away with it!

Andy had moved to Las Vegas by this time. I called him and got him involved in this situation. I felt the pressure not to be seen with the woman outside of official Palace Court supervision. I gave Andy instructions in Japanese to meet this woman with a handful of lawyers to discuss an agreement and legal representation. He did, and before the victim knew what was happening, she had signed her legal representation away to a local law firm and was flying to Boston, Massachusetts, to meet with a rape psychologist at Boston College, with a personal escort named Andy. Then she and Andy were off to New York, and from there, she left for Japan, and Andy returned to Las Vegas.

The pressures of the drama surrounding the rape case were heavy. One of my bosses took time to talk to me about his experience with what he called "real Vegas." I remember the day clearly, as he walked me down to his private parking spot beneath the hotel, sat me in his car, and said,

> Vegas has a corporate mafia that you should not mess with. When I first came here and began negotiating strategic contacts on behalf of the Palace Court Hotel

and Casino, I got in huge trouble. It had to do with a limo
contract and a powerful player in Vegas who owns one of
the largest fleets of limousines. I was looking to sign with
what I considered to be a better and more upright agency
when the owner of the losing firm lied to my superiors
and fabricated a scenario where it looked as though I was
trying to cheat the hotel. He came up with fake proof that
I had accepted a $10,000 bribe to sign with the competitor.
They threatened me, and I was forced to sign with the
worse deal and corrupt agency, but I tell you, the way they
twisted my arm in that situation scared the crap out of
me. I thought to myself, "These guys could have me killed
at the drop of a hat and not thought twice about it."

My boss looked at me with real concern in his eyes. I had a
good relationship with him, and I had shared with him that I had
mistranslated the message upper management told me to give to
the rape victim. The pressure got so heavy on me that a few friends
and I decided to get out of Vegas for a few days and let the whole
thing blow over. On a whim, four of us got on a plane and went to
Chicago for some rest and relaxation.

While I was in Chicago, Andy was flying all over America with
the victim. Her case had officially started. With the money that was
paid to Andy for escorting this woman everywhere, we decided
to start a business of our own called Wave International. It was
to be a translation business catering to the translation needs of
businesses. After incorporating ourselves legally, we focused on
growing the business.

As the year 2001 got underway, I felt a pull on my heart in a
different direction. To this day, I am not sure if the change of heart
was a product of the pressure of the rape fiasco getting to me, or
if my actions in taking the moral high ground were the cause. I
came to realize that what I had done for that rape victim was quite
possibly the first good and morally sound thing I had done for

anyone since moving to Vegas. The very decision to help her when it meant sticking my neck out was completely uncharacteristic for me at the time. It caused me to take a good look at who I had become ethically.

> *If I happened to get a girl pregnant as a result of a one-night stand, would I push for an abortion?*
> Yes, I would.
> *Would I go and pay for sex with a prostitute?*
> I already have. I paid for a prostitute in Tijuana, Mexico, more than a year ago.
> *Would I get drugs for a person if he offered me a $100 tip?*
> The answer was obvious ... yes.
> *And what about if he offered me a $20 tip?*
> Yes, I have sold drugs as an employee of the Palace Court for as little as a $20 tip.
> *Would I lie to my parents and loved ones about my life?*
> Yes, they have no idea of the corruption and filth I live in.
> *Do I laugh at the divorce rate in this country? Do I mock and say, "Vows are made to be broken"?*
> Yes, this is one of my many catch phrases, but suddenly, I failed to see the humor in it.

The internal debate of who I had become continued to rage for months as I looked at myself critically for the first time ever.

One day my boss came up to me and said, "Use our departmental phones with caution! I believe they have just been tapped by I.S. (Information Systems)." He looked at me sternly and then said, "This rape thing just got serious."

Paranoia was birthed that very day in my heart. Time passed, and one day I got a call on my cell phone from a friend within the ticket broker world who was affiliated with Broker B, the competitors of the broker agency with whom I had a conflict. This individual had been on the receiving end of my money scandal that attempted to financially break Broker A. By the time this phone call came in 2001, Broker A was continually losing money and beginning to suffer. This guy from Broker B sounded strange on the phone as he said, "Meet me tonight; I need to talk to you." I agreed and met him at a sushi joint to find out what was going on.

"Did you hear the news?" he started, as he looked at me with sternness.

"No, what news?" I asked.

"The news that Bob was murdered!" he said with stress.

Bob was a street runner who carried tickets from box office to broker and broker to buyer.

I was not catching the urgency, but I was saddened by the news. "I had not heard that," I said. "It's really too bad. Do you have any idea who did it?"

He slowly began to nod his head "yes," and the severity of it became clearer to me. "Broker A?" I asked.

"That's my guess. He has been watching money disappear for years now. The first assumption would be that a runner was pocketing it here and there and making his own deals on the side. How else could Broker A account for the fact that all the records are in order?"

"You're absolutely right," I said, as my heart began to pound. "Bob didn't have any known enemies around here, did he?"

"Not to my knowledge," he said. "Should we kill the scam?"

We talked on and on that evening, finally coming to the conclusion that if Broker A was actually Bob's murderer, and if they continued to see money vanish, they would realize that Bob had been the wrong target, but it would be futile to simply go on a killing spree. Though Broker A and B were competitors, there was no way to channel funds from one to another without a medium, so Broker B was really in no harm. If Broker A was able to pin the wrongdoing to one of the hotels, it would almost have to be a random selection of whom to point the finger at. There was a broad section of people who had made it quite clear that they despised the business tactics of Broker A. And I had maintained relationship with Broker A from the day I decided to break the firm financially to the day I found myself in that musky Japanese restaurant. What I had working for me was that I had done a stellar job in "keeping my friends close, but my enemies closer." Broker A certainly didn't like me, but there was no reason to assume I had been the cause of their vanishing money.

After mulling the scenario over until the wee morning hours, we left feeling somewhat secure. We continued the scam, and I followed through with my promise to break Broker A's financial bank as payback for screaming at me on the phone.

A few weeks passed with business as usual. Then one night I got a phone call on my cell phone from an unregistered number. I recognized the voice, though it sounded somewhat intoxicated. Chills went up my spine as I heard the slow slurs of drunkenness turn into an intelligible sentence. "I know you know about Bob. Now you should know, I know it was you. You're next." Before I could say anything, the phone went dead. "How in the world did he get my cell phone number?" I thought, as the slow but steady paranoia of my disintegrating life turned into outright panic. I was now being harassed on two fronts. First was from the Palace Court umbrella corporation as their suspicions of my personal involvement in the rape case grew. And now I was also being harassed from the ticket broker whom I had waged war against years earlier.

Many things happened as I faced the fear and anxiety of potentially being murdered. First, I felt a real threat over my life as the danger of whom I had managed to tick off in the Vegas corporate world hit me. I decided that it was time for me to get myself to a church, so that I might have a chance to make peace with God before being offed. To be honest, I had no idea where I was headed after death, given the conviction that I started feeling about my rebellious lifestyle. Next, the fear, worry, stress, and strife of my circumstances dramatically damaged my pursuit of pleasure.

I was feeling a lot of pain from my past bubble to the surface. I did not know how to deal with it, nor did I know from where it had come. I recklessly tried to squash it with acts of more horrific pleasure-seeking measures.

I suddenly began practicing a higher-stakes game of pleasure seeking. I received some weed from a fellow employee at the Palace Court, but waited for a night when I was alone in my house to smoke it. I viewed pornographic movies on an adult channel and masturbated. The feeling of masturbating, combined with the enhanced sensitivity of being high, gave me a rush that eased the pain—both from my past and from the conviction about my lifestyle. Following the usual pattern, the first experience felt the best. I recklessly pursued the intensity of that first feeling with every ensuing action. But the consequences increased as well. The sick and painful feeling I experienced each morning after I engaged in an act of lust left me yearning for even more to numb the pain.

During this season of fear and utter perversion, I had a strong hunger for the Bible. Instead of going out with friends to bars, restaurants, and clubs, I opted to stay home and read the Bible. The fascination of it gripped me in my pursuit to ease pain. Often, gross displays of lustful sin accompanied hours of Bible reading in the same night. The contradictions of my actions pursuing righteousness and acts of sin raged as I attempted to juggle the desires of my flesh and the spiritual truth. I had no idea what was going on with me, but stress and fear for my life continued to mount—I began waking up every morning believing that it may very well be my last day to live.

Life again sped up to an unhealthy pace, but this time nothing made sense. My life was a total and obvious display of hypocrisy. I was feeling real and positive emotions as I quietly sat and read the Word of God, and I was excited to tell people about it. But they often shunned me when they saw the contradiction of sin exhibited in my life.

For about two months, I told myself, "This week, I will go to church," but it never happened. Finally in March 2001, I woke up one Sunday morning and rebuked the excuses in my mind. I found a small Baptist church in Summerlin and walked in. The ushers greeted me warmly. The service was traditional, what I was used to. I have no idea what the seventy-five-year-old pastor talked about, but I was moved and gripped to the bone. It was as though he looked straight at me and held me out over hell on a rotten stick saying, "Change, son. Turn from your evil ways and find freedom from your bondage!" I walked out of church that day mesmerized with what I had heard. The pastor had spoken directly to me! I got to my car and unlocked the door to get in. I gazed one last time at the church building, and something happened for the first time in my life—I saw a vision.

In what can only be described as the "eye of my spirit," I saw the church building suddenly vanish. In its place stood numerous pillars made of beautiful stone and marble. The pillars stretched high into the sky, and they held up a large marble slate. There were probably twenty-five or thirty pillars, and the marble slate was huge and thick. It lay flat on all the pillars as a tabletop sits on the legs of a table. On it was written, "Life," and I knew that it was symbolic of my personal life. I gazed at the pillars and saw each one was assigned a specific word or phrase. One pillar was called, "Sin of Lust," another was labeled "Gluttony," and another "Greed." These pillars seemed untouchably powerful and strong. During this vision, I realized that God was showing me that my life was erected high on top of many pillars of sin, and I was further convicted by what the pastor had preached. Just before the vision ended, I saw a crack slice through the pillar closest to me. The slate of marble moved ever so slightly.

The vision ended, and I drove away from church with the conviction that my life needed to change. A glimmer of hope was ignited in my heart knowing that a change the size of a crack had penetrated the foundation of my sinful life! I decided right then that it was time for me to start walking down a different path.

WAR AND HYPOCRISY

13

The storm that leaves brokenness in its wake came out of nowhere in a horrific fury after I saw that first vision depicting sin as pillars of my life. From that moment, my social, physical, emotional, and spiritual worlds were flipped upside down and turned inside out. The quintessence of what made that year so difficult was the inaudible, indistinguishable, and unimaginably real war between:

1. My personal fear of man in the physical.
2. The fear of casting away my masks in the emotional.
3. My newly found fear of God in the spiritual.

I call it the war that births hypocrisy or God versus the devil for the heart of man.

My rebellious lifestyle in Las Vegas climaxed when I reached a place of "do-or-die." As stress mounted, I honestly believed that the single imperative in my life was to find some truth about God now because I might not be alive tomorrow. In desperation I was ready to sacrifice my reckless pursuit of pleasure to find the truth about God! I chose to stay home and read the Bible instead of partying and pursuing a life of sin.

I opened up a battlefield within me that said, "My heart is up for grabs!" to anyone listening in the spiritual world. I exercised my God-given right to free choice and opened a Pandora's box in the spiritual by showing, through spending time in prayer, that the debate about the legitimacy of God in my life was not over. As the foundations of my life were shaken to their core, I was propelled to search for truth. Now I can say with utter confidence that I serve a God who gladly wages war for my heart, mind, and soul. For many years, I grossly misunderstood this concept and was totally incapable of seeing God in this light.

The fear for my security and safety was real. I was the ruler and conqueror of my existence up until 2001, but, as I lost control over my destiny and fell into the hands of known killers, I became petrified with fear. The pressures and stress mounted on me to a nearly intolerable level. I was scared that man would murder me for the crimes I had committed, and I feared that the rumor of hell might actually be true! In my fuzzy understanding of life, death, and spirituality, I figured that if hell does exist, the critical imperative is to seek some truth about God. So, my fear of man created a fear of hell that led to a struggle beyond my wildest expectations. In the act of juggling these two fears, I set in motion horrible contradictory actions and a season of blatant hypocrisy.

Here is an example of this dualistic existence:

One day a casino host at the Palace Court asked me to phone a big mafia boss in Japan to invite him to a midsummer party, which the Palace Court wished to throw for some of the more high-profile gamblers. I did, and the man arrived a few months later in great anticipation and excitement. The Palace Court then told me, "You will need to attend this party with the Japanese gentleman. You are his contact, and you must cater to his needs."

The conflict was on: My heart was burning for a different life, a life outside of this continual disregard for morality. I knew what the party would consist of—sex and drugs. My utter fear of man still talked me into participating in these actions, though I was excited and passionate about the bits of truth I was finding in the Bible and at church. I was excited about my spiritual awakening and eagerly talked with people about what was going on in my heart, but my actions took me to the prevalent midsummer party. In action, I often contradicted what I preached.

I had serious doubts about whether or not I should attend the party because my involvement would be a direct contradiction to what I knew was morally right for me. I thought about calling in sick or making up a story about my car not starting. In the end, I chose to go because I was scared that the Palace Court might put more pressure on me if I didn't. I cost them a grip of money with the lawsuit I had initiated over the rape case. For my own security, I felt I needed to cater to this mafia boss from Japan.

The party was a classic Vegas scene. We congregated in a large suite on the top floor of the hotel, and soon the women were brought in. Each gambler was invited to take a girl or two for himself and was told that the first round of conventional sex was on the hotel, but everything after, or "extra," had to be paid by the individual patron. The men chose their women, and instant couples were formed. From the suite, we all got into a gigantic limo and went to Lake Mead where a nice boat was waiting for us. We boarded, and I was not surprised to find cocaine displayed with a beautiful welcome sign that read: "Welcome to the party of midsummer, provided by the Palace

Court." Corruption reigns in Las Vegas.

The boat slowly eased away from the dock, and the women promptly took off their clothing. Orgies of creative perversion were happening all over the boat. My Japanese mafia boss quickly passed out in the main cabin from too much champagne and cocaine. I found myself wondering. "What am I doing here?"

I was content to allow the sickening display of lust to continue on the boat, while I swam in the warm water and nursed an ice-cold beer. I had no desire to participate in the sex and drugs, though they asked me to join in many times. There were always notable names at these Vegas parties, many of whom I was surprised to see doing such things, but even pressure from the celebrities in attendance didn't succeed in talking me into the sin this time.

As the party drew to an end and the sun set over the lake, we got back into the limo and drove to the hotel. I made a decision right then to never again take part in such a party. It was at that moment that the fear of God surpassed the fear I felt toward man.

As a result of that decision, it seemed like the devil kicked up his efforts for my heart, and the war continued to rage. Casting away my masks created a terrible battle. As my fear of God and man ignited the search to know more about God's truth, He began to take me backward in time. In my quiet place before God, I understood that as He was able to draw nearer to me, the more I was willing to uncover deep recesses of hurt and allow Jesus' blood to wash over them—healing my wounds and giving my distorted pain perspective a more truthful and accurate focus.

I was scared to death of reliving my painful past. I often made up good excuses of why I should not cast away my masks. Quiet times were fearful for me when I began to understand that God was real and that He wanted a relationship with me. It became clear that this relationship could only be birthed in the "shadow of the valley of death."

The process of reliving pain, recalling hurtful memories, and weeping over issues that I never allowed myself the liberty to embrace before became what I call the Years of Emergence. This season of emergence began soon after the midsummer party, around August 2001, and has gone on ever since, but the most intense years were between New Year's Eve 2001 and New Year's Eve 2003. The Years of Emergence have largely consisted of the ups and downs of life as a bondservant of the Lord. These years have seen relational growth and have consisted of wonderfully rich and terribly dry spiritual times. Through the experiences, I have come to know some of my true identity—who the Lord intended me to be when He formed me in my mother's womb. These years have often been painful, and many tears have been shed over the truths that I learned. The process redefined the essence of my understanding of spiritual warfare and equipped me to take part in some spiritual conflicts. Understanding the nature of spiritual warfare continues to be a learning and growing process for me, and I am sure it always will.

Everything that happened in 2001 played a part in the breaking of my emotional, physical, and spiritual life. My friends could not understand why I was changing, and I wasn't sure how to explain it to them. I tried to show excitement about the reality of God's love ... and though my excitement was real, at night my friends still saw me getting involved in explicit acts of sin and defilement. My ever-changing opinions about the nature of Christ failed to carry any weight because it was evident that I did not believe or live the basics of what I preached.

One example of my compromising lifestyle was the "girlfriend" I had during the first half of 2001. She and I were nothing more than sexual partners, and we never had an honest and deep conversation. Everyone around us probably knew it. I had grown accustomed to finding security in immoral relationships, so the process of giving that up took some time.

My hypocrisy hurt my relationships with both the sinful and righteous crowds. I became more depressed and broken over my inability to juggle all three elements of war: fear of God, fear of man, and fear of showing my real self by casting away the false identities of my masks. The immoral sexual relationships I had during this period were a product of the choices I continued to make to live under the deceptive masks of hurt. The hypocrisy reigned and redefined who I was. My identity before others was up into the air, as one day I would be on a God kick and the next day I would be smoking dope. It was a never-ending cycle, and my life was becoming more broken by the minute.

What many acquaintances did not understand was that I also hated the hypocrisy in my life, but I was too scared to simply dump the sin and evil all at once. I now understand that this type of radical change rarely happens overnight. In fact, in that early phase of attempting to transition from the way of sin to the way of His will, there was a Bible-thumping, religious community of people that identified themselves as Christians who really hurt me with their inability to distinguish spiritual immaturity from rebellion. I was a spiritual infant, but I felt like the Christian community expected me to perform at a fifth-grade level.

September 11, 2001, created a financial crisis in tourist destinations such as Las Vegas, and every inhabitant of Las Vegas felt the sting. I had grown accustomed to a very extravagant lifestyle that mandated a steady and powerful flow of finances. When they stopped coming in, I fell into debt. But September 11th was but a small piece of the overall assault on my financial world. The business that Andy and I had created was not doing well, and a few of our investments failed. Though we had our own business, we still held other jobs, but suddenly Andy lost his. We could not afford our home/office, and a great deal of expenses started to roll onto my credit cards. The financial struggle erected a barrier between Andy and me relationally—to the point that we were not talking to one another.

The pressures continued to mount, and I began to search for a way out of Las Vegas. I considered a possible return to Woodland Park, but I was falling too far, too fast into debt, and the economy of Woodland Park (or Colorado Springs for that matter) could not possibly sustain the consequences of my lifestyle. On top of consumer debt, I had ceased going to UNLV the semester before and was paying on student loans. There was no way I could make it all work.

I continued to search for a way to leave Vegas, but every time a possibility arose, I was faced with the same truth: I could not afford to go anywhere. As I prayed and hoped for a way out, a glimmer of hope came from a conversation I had with my parents. In late August my mom phoned. "We have news for you," she said with excitement in her voice.

"What is it?" I asked.

"Well, Dad and I are thinking about moving to Afghanistan!" she said, as I about dropped the phone.

"What? Where did this come from?" I asked in shock, and she explained.

After she finished the story of why they were contemplating Afghanistan, I asked in complete seriousness, "Can I go with you? Please, you need to take me with you! I have to get out of here, and I can't tell you how much this is resounding in my heart right now!" I was almost afraid to believe this could be an option out of Vegas.

Toward the end of that conversation, my mom revealed, "Well, we're really not in a place to be able to go for about a year, so we're waiting for the Lord's confirmation. But if you're interested, you should pursue it for yourself!"

Through the next few months, I looked into the prospect of going to Afghanistan, and my folks set me up with their contact at Shelter for Life (SFL), an aid organization. Dialogue began, and my hope slowly grew.

Throughout 2001, I felt like I was on a roller-coaster ride. Each time I hit the pit of despair, life picked up just enough to sink me further down the next time around. In December, the final blow that broke my world came. I got a ticket for having an expired license plate on my car. I thought, "No problem, I'll simply go and renew it." Upon arriving at the DMV, I was told, "Sir, you have never owned registration on your car. All I see is registration on your motorcycle, and so I'm going to have to charge you $1,400 for the fines and fees." I was in utter shock and disbelief. I showed the lady behind the counter my proof of registration, but for some reason the only registration they had on record was for my motorcycle. I had to pay the cost of what I continue to believe was an attack of the enemy and a DMV screw-up. With tears in my eyes, I walked out of the DMV and went home completely broke.

That was the last straw. I felt totally out of control. I could not smile, talk, laugh, or enjoy anything. I heard the whispers of deception say, "Look, you have not been in this much pain since Japan, a time when you were supposedly trusting in God. Why live this way? Go back to enjoying life and get yourself out of this mode once and for all. The way to the life you once had is refusing Jesus as your Lord." The whispers were enticing, and I would be lying if I said I didn't listen and consider the option. But I also was afraid of the wrath of God on the Day of Judgment, which seemed too close for comfort.

December 24, 2001, I got off work and followed my normal routine: I went straight to the bar. My friend and colleague met me there, and I drank like I had never had a drink before. I got so drunk that I slept through Christmas Day and woke up the next day feeling as low as I had ever felt.

The night of December 28, I left my apartment and walked down to the interstate with the intention of jumping into the traffic and ending it all. I got to the bridge with the busy highway beneath and took a few deep breaths. I thought, "Do I have the guts?" The answer was frighteningly sober and felt very resolute, "Yes, I do."

Then I asked myself, "Do I have the will?" and this time the answer did not come.

I was frustrated that SFL had seemingly put me on the back burner, and I faced the real prospect that I might remain in Vegas for yet another year! I was tired of looking over my shoulder; I was tired of the temptations to participate in sin; I was tired of losing everything I had worked so hard for in wealth, identity, and friend-ships. What was the point of the life I had found in Vegas? Did I have the will to end it? The answer was "no."

As I stepped away from the edge of the bridge, I cried bitterly and threw my hands up in the air and shouted, "I give up! Kill me. End my life if you will. I hate it anyway! I hate my pain, and I hate my life. I cannot juggle God and this world, and I now know that the two cannot be mixed ... so do with me as you will. I quit."

I did not know whom I was madder at: God, the devil, or myself. That night I let everything that I had been juggling come crash-ing down. I surrendered lordship of my life to whomever wanted it. I did not even care who, as long as it was not me, because I was sufficiently aware that I had done nothing since moving to Vegas to better myself. I was a total wreck spiritually, emotionally, and physically. I was tired of trying to make my life work.

Earlier, I mentioned that the Years of Emergence were most in-tense between New Year's Eve of 2001 and 2003. Well, New Year's Eve of '01 was upon me. Little did I know that the most significant and powerful spiritual death and rebirth of my young existence was approaching. Some friends had come from out of town to enjoy the Las Vegas New Year's Eve celebration. We were on the strip await-ing the countdown to the New Year. Though the strip was crowded, it seemed somewhat sparse compared to previous years, as the aftermath of September 11th continued to linger in the hearts of many, and some were concerned about the possibility of an attack on Las Vegas during New Year's Eve. The midnight hour drew near. I was not drinking because of the lagging uneasiness in my stomach at the very thought of alcohol after my Christmas Eve binge.

The countdown started, and a most odd feeling came over me. Time slowed to a creep as the crowd chanted the numbers in descending order from ten to one. I started to cry. What was I crying about? I cried harder and knelt to one knee. With my head down, I cried tears of joy because I knew that the struggle and strife of the past year was over and done. I felt the unexplainable love of something greater than myself fall upon me, and the warmth of it induced a steady stream of tears. I felt the words in my heart say, "It is over; you have summitted the mountain, and the harsh ascent is over. Rest in My love."

The moment ended, and I got up and looked around to see thousands of drunks. The reality of what I had just felt on the strip was more real than anything I had ever experienced before in my pursuit of pleasure. It felt immeasurably better than any high I had ever had. Somehow I knew my life was changed forever, and peace took over the very essence my being. It is impossible to put into words, but the love and joy I felt on Las Vegas Boulevard that night changed my very perspective of life. I was no longer scared for my life. I was no longer afraid of people's opinion of me. And I no longer felt anger toward the life I endured in Japan. Everything about my perspective of life completely changed!

A few years later, the Lord told me what was happening in the spiritual world that generated what I felt physically and emotionally. I felt the affirming love of my heavenly Father pour over me amidst thousands of drunkards as the blood of Christ poured over my pain perspective. The blood of His sacrifice on the cross birthed a new reality for me, one that has remained the backbone of my life ever since—the reality that Christ came and died on the cross to redeem my pain.

I had not, at the time, formally asked the Lord back into my life, nor had I asked His forgiveness for the rebuke I gave Him when I first moved to Las Vegas. To be honest, I had completely forgotten that I ever told God to go away. However, in my pursuit of His kingdom in 2002, I prayed and talked to God as though I had never banished Him from my life. He honored me in that pursuit, and He revealed His love for me on the Las Vegas strip on December 31, 2001. To this day, it remains one of the most powerful experiences of my life.

Ironically, a few days later I was called by SFL and commissioned to go to Afghanistan as a U.S. aid worker for a six-month assignment. Within what seemed like the blink of an eye, I was north-bound on I-15 out of town.

CHANGING PERSPECTIVES

14

I was so wrapped up in the fear and stress of life in Las Vegas, that the first time I stopped to imagine what it would be like to live in Afghanistan was on the highway as I drove toward Colorado. My plan was to spend a few days in Colorado saying goodbye to my parents, and then fly from Denver to Chicago, Chicago to London, London to Istanbul, and finally Istanbul to Dushanbe, the capital city of Tajikistan. Once I arrived in Dushanbe, I planned on spending a few days at the SFL regional headquarters, then driving down to the southern border and crossing into Afghanistan by foot. As I flew east, the trip had a James Bond feel to it—I had very little information about anything other than the general plan of departures and arrivals. I had no idea who would meet me at the airport, what my job would entail in Afghanistan, what I was supposed to bring, or what I was doing with my life in general.

In late March 2002, I boarded the airplane in Istanbul, Turkey. It was destined for Dushanbe, a four-hour flight. There was no seat assignment, and I quickly realized that the passenger jet was actually half full of cargo. The flight attendant motioned for me to sit down in a seat, and soon the jet was taxiing to the runway. My heart began to pound hard in my chest as I realized that the seat which I was sitting on was not affixed to the floor of the cabin in any way. I may as well have been sitting on a folding chair! There were people lying down in the aisle, people chatting while standing up, and a general feeling of chaos during the takeoff. It was evident that safety precautions are nonexistent in this area of the world.

The plane arrived in Dushanbe at 4:30 a.m. We disembarked the aircraft just in time to see a hint of light come over the horizon. The passengers were led by Russian soldiers carrying AK-47 assault weapons to a small room made from what looked like tinfoil. There was one dim light in the small rectangular room. We all huddled inside, shivering from the cold, and waited. We remained in that room for three hours until finally our number was called and we were ushered into a new room. Next, the KGB questioned us about our purpose for being in Tajikistan. The guy was pleasant, but obviously not in any hurry to get us through customs (and I thought government workers were slow in America). We gained new perspectives quickly on this trip!

I spent the next week getting to know the SFL staff working in Dushanbe. I met with the head of the office, learned what I would be doing in Afghanistan, recovered from the jetlag, and acclimated to the slow-paced life of Tajikistan. Prior to my arrival in Dushanbe, SFL personnel had told me, "Dushanbe is similar to the United States, or any other Western country, compared to Afghanistan." This statement seemed largely unbelievable as I walked to an Internet café one evening to check my email. "This is nothing like America," I thought, as I dodged open manholes, hid from packs of wild dogs, heard screaming and yelling, and did everything in my power not to make eye contact with the drunken Russian solders who terrorized the Tajik citizens. Corruption, violence, and a rotten smell permeated the air. Almost all the buildings looked identical—large, bland, block-style, cement structures. There were also a large number of buildings that were abandoned long ago, halfway through construction. The Russian industry had disappeared after the fall of Communism, and Tajikistan became a sovereign state. It seemed to me that if Tajikistan was its own independent state, they were still being manipulated and governed by the intimidation tactics of the Russians. I did my best to keep my head down and stay away from negativity.

The statement about Dushanbe being comparable to a Western city made sense as we drove four hours south to the Afghan border a few days later. In March 2002, there were no commercial airlines flying into Afghanistan because of the bombing campaigns that the United States and its coalition were performing against the Taliban. The only way into the country was over a physical border. My point of entry was the Tajik/Afghan border. As we drew near, the road largely disappeared, and I found myself bouncing up and down inside the little Jeep as it made its way over some very rough terrain. Little did I know, I would not be enjoying the luxury and smoothness of pavement for quite some time.

The border was nothing but a dry wasteland—a desert with a large river called the Amu Darya flowing through it. The river represented the actual borderline. On the Tajik side, there were a dozen solders with assault weapons standing by, doing nothing, and quite evidently bored out of their minds. Our driver was speaking to them as they checked our bags and papers. Then we were led down to the shore of the river, and I watched as a large raft linked to a mechanical pulley system came across from the Afghan side to pick us up. Evidently, this was the main way into the country. The raft was large enough to carry two fully loaded Kamaz dump trucks. My fellow aid workers and I got onto the raft and sailed into Afghanistan.

The raft docked on the Afghan shore, and we carried our bags off. The Tajik driver who had brought us to the border was not allowed to cross the river, so two other Americans and I were left to fend for ourselves. Quickly, a number of turbaned, rag-wearing Afghan men came up to us and spoke in a very strange-sounding language; we had no idea what they were saying. One of the local project managers named John was supposed to meet us at the border, but he was running late. So for the time being, we tried to keep the atmosphere causal and pretended we had a clue as to what the Afghan border personnel were saying. Through internationally understood gestures, I came to realize that the Afghans were looking to get paid off.

John finally showed up wearing the same rags and sandals that the Afghans were wearing and exchanged pleasantries with them. He went from one border guy to another, hugging each one of them and speaking to them in Dari. He had a beard and looked just like one of the locals. Soon, he made his way toward us and said, "Hey, guys, sorry I'm late." This statement caught me off guard, and was both surprising and comforting, as the South Carolinian good-ol'-boy accent brought back a sense of familiarity. John had spent years in Afghanistan by the time I arrived there, and he had grown accustomed to the life, way, and customs of the Afghan people. John had been there in the heat of Taliban brutality and during the U.S.-led bombing campaigns.

The border personnel were adamant about us paying them a fee for crossing, so a debate was sparked between John and the chief in charge of the border on the Afghan side. It lasted for what seemed like an eternity, as both sides were unwilling to budge. The desert sun was hot, and soon tea was brought out as the debate raged on. I finally said, "Hey, John, we have money budgeted for them. What are they asking for?"

"Twenty dollars," John said, "but it's not right for them to bribe us, so I'm going to talk them out of it."

The debate continued, until finally John lost, and we each paid $20 to cross. Soon after arriving in Dushanbe, I realized that corruption and bribery are a way of Central Asian life.

We drove away from the border, and a few minutes later John said, "We're coming into the city of Dasht-I-Qala. We have an office here and are doing some projects from this location. You'll be responsible for this region." I looked around to see men and boys and a few little girls idling on the side of the road, but in no way did this look like a city. It looked more like heaps of ruins than actual neighborhoods. Once in a while, we saw the ghostly figure of a woman walk by. Women were covered from head to toe in a flowing sheet called a *burka*. It was a strange sight to behold.

We drove for another three hours over a very bumpy road to a town called Rustaq—the place I called home for the next six months. The evening was upon us, and, soon after arriving in Rustaq, we ate a bit of mutton and made our way to the SFL guesthouse, my residence, about a five-minute walk from the office. The guesthouse, office, and every other structure in Rustaq were made of mud and sun-dried brick. There was no electricity, running water, heat, gas, or anything else I was used to in Vegas. There were all sorts of livestock roaming the streets but almost no vehicles. People rode donkeys as the primary means of travel. There was really no such thing as a city economy, for the economy was the four aid organizations that had a presence in Rustaq. There were roughly 20,000 people in Rustaq, and they were all, in one way or another, affiliated with one of the aid organizations.

After living in the luxury of Vegas, the physical changes I underwent while in Afghanistan were immense and terribly difficult on my body. When I arrived in Rustaq, I was five foot eight and weighed 215 pounds. When I left Afghanistan six months later, I weighed around 150. Probably four of the six months that I lived in Afghanistan were spent with horrible stomach illnesses, some of which are recurring and continue to bother me today. Showers were a luxury not a right, so I adapted to being filthy all the time as well as to always smelling the very strong body odor of others. My diet of expensive food and drink suddenly changed, and I was forced to eat mutton and beans every single day for six months. The region where I lived was extremely poor, even by Afghan standards, and imports were very hard to come by. It took me about six weeks to finally talk a shopkeeper into bringing Nescafé coffee into town for a little variance from the ever-prevalent black or green tea.

I missed drinking ice-cold beer. I missed conversations. I missed watching football on TV. I missed my friends and family, and loneliness set in hard. There was so much time to sit and think in Afghanistan. Life moves at a very slow pace, and it is not unusual, but quite normal, to see men and boys sitting around drinking tea for hours on end. I was uncomfortable with having so much time on my hands; my life in Vegas was so fast-paced that I never had time to sit and think ... but in Afghanistan, thinking was all I could do to keep from dying of boredom. This is not to say that we were bored during work, for there was plenty for us to do. But the stillness and quietness of the land was eerie by night as I sat for hours simply thinking, pondering, remembering.

I felt totally safe in Afghanistan, though I admit that I wet myself the first time I heard the whistle of a bullet go past. SI had an unexplainable sense of being perfectly situated in the Lord's will, and I felt absolutely sure that, in life or death, I was where I needed to be. By day, I worked and did my part in the facilitation of our USAID-funded projects, and by night, I tossed and turned in anguish from the illnesses that pounded my stomach.

People stared at me in Afghanistan, similar to the way folks stared at me in Japan. But in Afghanistan, the stares were never followed by laughter. Rather, they seemed to represent genuine curiosity and often a sense of gratitude. The people were very kind to me too. I soon found that the general population in Afghanistan was very grateful for the actions of America and the West and the war we waged against the Taliban.

The crowds, however, took some getting used to. Each time my vehicle stopped, a crowd of anywhere from fifty to a few hundred men and boys gathered around and stared. If conversation was ever initiated, they talked, sometimes for hours, and sounded off about what needs might be met to better the lives of the citizens of that particular village. It was quite clear that the average Afghan viewed me and the other Western aid workers as walking dollar signs. In truth, I was filthy rich compared to every one of them.

Some of the emotional changes associated with life in Afghanistan came from the sheer magnitude of suffering I had to witness on a daily basis. In Vegas, I would get mad when some idiot cut me off while I zipped down the interstate on my way to work. But in Afghanistan, a new anger burned within me as I saw countless instances of injustice. Time and again I witnessed atrocities and was obliged to sit by and be a spectator though my heart raged. Kids dying, landslides taking out entire villages, bombs falling on innocent civilians, and militia who believe themselves to be above the law of human dignity raping and murdering at will.

One day, my small convoy drove from one project site to another, taking pictures of the progress to report back to USAID. After the inspections, we started the long drive home but chose to go a different way. Instead of going south and then west back to Rustaq, we chose to go north and then west via Dasht-I-Qala. In a small village east of Dasht-I-Qala, I noticed a young boy, about ten years old, limping along the shoulder of the road. He looked beat up. I asked the driver to stop, and my chief of staff named Maboobulah and I hopped out of the vehicle. I asked the boy to come over to me; Maboob translated. The boy came, and true to form, a great crowd gathered to see what was going on. The boy had a huge gash across the left side of his shaved head, stretching from just above the left eye and ending behind the left ear. I told Maboob to ask the mob what had happened to the boy, and an older gentleman stepped forward with the story.

The boy's father had passed away a year earlier, and this was the eldest male in the household. The boy was doing labor here and there to support his mother and siblings. Times became so desperate that he began stealing food from the local shopkeeper in order to sustain his family. This had been going on for some time. Then one day the shopkeeper caught the boy in the act and had chased him away, and the boy had taken a fall as he ran. This had happened a few days ago, according to the storytelling graybeard. Silence came over the crowd as I gently tilted the boy's head toward me and noticed small white worms crawling inside the gaping wound on his head. The boy began to cry softly.

"Why did his mother not dress this wound?" I asked, and the man told me that the mother had passed away the same day that the boy fell. The boy started crying more openly. Then the man told me that the boy's siblings were with a relative who was very poor, and that there was no money for the boy to receive medical treatment.

Somehow, I knew that the story of this lad falling down while being chased was a lie, and I had a feeling that the mother was probably killed for the boy's actions. I felt like screaming! My heart was yelling, "What injustice is this that a young boy gets beat up for trying to get food for his widowed mother and younger siblings, and his mother is killed for the act of robbery!" The child was limping, but I couldn't tell what other bruises and cuts he had on his little body. I then looked at Maboob and said, "Translate this word for word to these people."

"Who among you believes himself to be upright before God?" I asked. They all looked at me eagerly as Maboob translated, but no one moved.

"Will the man who is moral and upright before your Allah step forward, because I have a favor to ask of you." With that, an older man who was evidently reputable within the community came forward and introduced himself. I nodded and pulled out my money and said, "Take this child to the pharmacy. Tell the shopkeeper to dress this wound, cleaning it out and killing these worms." I said this to the old man as I pointed to the worms crawling around in the gash.

"Here is the money that you will need to pay for it," I said, as I handed him a wad of cash. "There should be plenty left over after all the expenses are paid." The man nodded his understanding. I then handed the boy a wad of money and said, "This is for you to take to your relative. Give it to him for the added responsibility of you and your siblings." Then, looking back at the old man, I said, "Walk with this boy to make sure he takes this money to his relative."

The old man then asked what he should do with the remainder of the money after paying the expenses at the pharmacy, and I told him to keep it. He thanked me and promised to do exactly as instructed, and I went away with a broken heart and a new understanding about the God I serve.

The God I serve cares about the lowest of the low, and He cares deeply for the young boy who had most assuredly lost all hope of joy in life. I would not be surprised if the boy had, just prior to my vehicle driving past, prayed that he would be taken care of, and God answered him by using me. I remember tears in my eyes all the way back to Rustaq that day as I came to a greater understanding of the love that our God has for His beloved creation.

I was emotional as I realized that God loves me just the same as He does the hurting child. In my mind, a new value was placed on human life, and I ached for the needless death that happens each and every day to thousands of people all over the world. God cares about each aborted baby in America; He cares about the parentless child in Afghanistan; He cares about the little girl sold into pornography in Thailand. I realized for the first time that God cares more than I could ever know!

Most of the time in Afghanistan, I felt like an observer when the atrocities of life stung the local Afghan people, but once in a while the Lord used me to bring relief. Knowing that I made a difference brought some of the most powerful and joyful feelings I have ever experienced. In all honesty, I received much more than any good I could have hoped to bring to the Afghan people. I now realize that my changing perspectives were all part of God's plan in leading me to Afghanistan. After returning to the States, I was humbled to understand that, from God's perspective, Afghanistan was more about my growth in Him than it was about my ability to save others. Though I longed to be the hero when pain and suffering arose, God simply wanted to get to know me and to reveal Himself to me in loving relationship.

However, while going through the day-to-day monotony of life in Afghanistan and spending countless hours in quiet solitude, I admit that God's will was anything but clear to me. I went through various seasons of questions, opinions, and thoughts about who God is and what He stands for. There were many nights that I cursed God for my own lack of understanding about why He allowed this palpable suffering to continue. I went through a season where the weight of condemnation was exceedingly heavy for the life of sin I lived in Vegas and a season where the shame of my past paralyzed me from praying or reading the Bible at all.

The primary spiritual perspective change that I underwent while living in Afghanistan was in my understanding of Christ. One night, as the guilt of my past was hindering any attempt to pray or read the Bible, I fell to my knees and realized truth. The overwhelming feelings came abruptly, and I began to sob. I felt a strong presence say, "Talk with Me, be with Me, sing with Me, dance with Me, for all I want is you! I don't care about the past, I don't care about your works, I don't care about your sins. I only care about being with you! If it was not this big of a deal to Me, I would not have died on the cross for you!"

I was besieged with raw, emotional, heartfelt truths about the price God paid on the cross to have a relationship with me. God died for me so that I could be with Him. God died for the redemption of my rebellions, but over and over, my pride hindered the relationship from going anywhere. God literally hurts at the prospect of not being with me in intimacy. As I remained distanced from the Lord, under the condemnation of my past, God longed to sit, talk, dance, sing, and be intimate with me, but all I could focus on were my own shortcomings. I came to a dramatic realization that condemnation is nonexistent in the kingdom of God. Every moment I spent sulking over my horrific past was a moment that I was missing with my loving Lord.

Physically, emotionally, and spiritually, my life dramatically changed in Afghanistan. Slowly, I realized one truth about God, and another would follow it. With each revelation of deeper understanding, I found a hunger for the knowledge of the Lord growing within my heart. The more I learned about the true God of love, my pain perspective became less distorted and more accurate. I saw my past life in a clearer and more truthful light. I hurt less on the inside as the old pain perspective was traded in for a new perspective rooted in pure love. Afghanistan will always be one of the most cherished seasons of my life, despite the ups and downs of growing pains and changing perspectives.

MY NEW

PERSPECTIVE
OF GOD

15

While living in Las Vegas, I used to see life through the lens of my surroundings. I understood life to be a system where men and women wake up, go to work, make their money, enjoy their money, and do more of the same. Stress was usually an insignificant irritation I felt toward the prospect of not being able to have what I wanted—like a new car, vacations, time off work, a day at the spa, a round of golf. My perspective changed somewhat as stress was redefined in 2001, when I began to fear for my life.

But the bulk of my altered perspective was realized during my time in Afghanistan, where stress is lived in the milieu of literal hardship. Only after living in Afghanistan did I understand that, for the majority of the world's population, stress is defined and lived out in not having food to eat or clothes to wear, being shot and killed for no legitimate reason, being raped or molested, and suffering the pain and hurts of others. In Las Vegas, each rising sun represented a new day full of new opportunities for me to experience the pleasures of my heart. For the vast majority of men and women in Afghanistan, each sunrise and the 5:00 a.m. call to prayer represents a new day full of challenges, hardships, and questions as to where the day's provisions might come from.

In contemplating the disparity of life between Afghanistan and America, I saw how the world could easily view our society as arrogant and stuck-up, living in a bubble, and basking in a false sense of security. As I watched a broader perspective of life unfold, I had conflicting feelings toward my "home," the United States of America. Part of me felt America was home, but another part of me did not.

Before moving to Afghanistan, I used to proclaim that places like that "ought to become nuclear test sites." Though I never really felt included as an American, I was caught up in a ridiculous amount of national pride. After living in Afghanistan, I now enjoy America and the luxuries that it has to offer with a new appreciation, and I have a more sober outlook about the issue of our perceived national security.

Another perspective that changed for me was in the way I viewed women. I had been so hurt by women throughout my life that the first time I saw a woman in a burka in Afghanistan, I was numb to the pain that she had to live with day by day. Thoughts crept into my mind like, "I would love for a feminist in the States to see this ... then she might understand where her political agenda could potentially end up!" I wanted to pat the first Afghan man I saw on his back and say, "Good for you! America needs a dose of your strong-arm tactic in dealing with women who get out of line."

In the States, we tend to make sport of male-female competition. While I lived in rebellion, I took part in this gender war on a regular basis. There are rivalries in the work place, in schools, in the family unit between spouses, between siblings, and now we can boast same-sex relational wars with the issue of gay-and-lesbian marriage catching the media's eye.

Coming from America's outlook on gender differences, one

might be able to see where my horrific legitimations of the gross violation of Afghan women's rights came from. I am a product of pain by definition of being human on planet earth. I am also a product of a society that tells me not to deal with the pain, but instead to make sport of it, bypass it, go around it, repress it, or pretend it doesn't exist. In not dealing with my issues of pain, and in this case my painful past associated with women, I was prone to a very distorted and ugly perspective of women as a whole. More than anything else, my perspective changed through realizing that the issues I had with women were not so much about "them," but rather "me."

Before Afghanistan, I was in camp "men" and they were in camp "women," and strife and competition existed between them and us. I did not see myself, or the other men in my camp, as coheirs to the problem of gender-related issues until an interesting conversation I had with Maboob one afternoon during lunch. We were quietly eating and watching BBC World when a thought-provoking story came on about divorce. The investigative reporter covered the growing epidemic of divorce in America and claimed that some 60 percent of all marriages fail in the United States. This statistic shocked Maboob, and we got into a good, long discussion about it. He asked why fellow faith-driven men and women, Christians, were not able to follow through with their vow to God. I said that I did not know. The BBC reporter had made some claims about the incredibly high divorce rate among Christian couples, as well. Maboob told me that it is very unusual for Afghans to divorce. "Probably less than 10 percent of us will ever divorce. We have a more proper fear of God maybe." Maboob made a good point, and I agree in many ways.

The conversation made me think, though, and in my meditation about the issue of divorce and gender wars, I saw America's epidemic as a joint male-female issue of hurt and pain. Men blame women for not living within the context of their roles as wives, mothers, and nurturers; women blame men for not living within the context of their roles as providers, husbands, and fathers. My conclusion was that men are just as much to blame for our reprehensible and rapidly decaying social existence in America as women are. I hurt for the women wearing burkas and tried to understand the fear and pain they must have to deal with every day of their lives. I then transferred that limited understanding to women in America, and feminists suddenly became my equal. Women—traditionalists and feminists alike—are the same as me in terms of pain, struggle, confusion, and hurt. A few days after that BBC World news report on divorce, I reopened the conversation with Maboob and said, "I think I can point to why America has such a bad divorce rate."

"Why is that?" he asked.

"Because we live in a world where it is painful to admit wrong."

"What do you mean?" he said with a puzzled look.

"Let me ask you this," I began, trying to create an analogy for him. "Why is it that Afghan men require their women to wear the burka?"

"Well, there are issues with their dignity," he replied, "and we are required not to lust over the body of females, as it is prohibited in our faith."

"Exactly." I said, "The men cover the women up because they lust. The problem is not in how God created the woman, and in the fact that she resembles beauty, but rather the problem is that men are not able to refrain from lusting, which is a disgrace before God. My point about America and the divorce rate is that we live in a world where it hurts to admit wrong or fault. Just like in Afghanistan, men in America blame the women for problems that have nothing to do with them, and the women blame the men. There are always two sides to every story, but the problem in America is that each side believes they are justified and right. I used to think that the women were crazy, and now I am starting to understand that maybe we all are crazy."

My perspectives continued to change and become redefined as

strange experiences, coupled with a lot of time to think, propelled my critical and questioning heart.

Before I knew it, I was flying out of Dushanbe, Tajikistan, in route to Istanbul, Turkey, for a week of rest and relaxation before my return to America. The Afghan episode had left me a changed person. I was fifty pounds smaller, but the physical changes were not the most noticeable differences. I was more reserved and less overt and in your face. My pride existed, as it does today, but it was crippled by my experiences there. I shed the chip on my shoulder, as one friend defined it. In every way, I was a completely different person in how I spoke and related to others.

I decided to move home to Woodland Park and finish my degree in Colorado. I had no interest in moving back to Las Vegas, and I knew that my folks would soon be moving to Afghanistan, so I had a place to myself in Colorado. I was looking forward to opening a new chapter in my life. A friend's mom was looking into school opportunities for me, and I was eager to settle down in a quiet place and delve into the intricacy and beauty of this new friend of mine, Jesus Christ.

Culture shock hit me again as I walked down one of many corridors in London's Heathrow Airport on my way home, trying to make a transfer flight that would carry me to Chicago's O'Hare Airport. As I shuffled through the terminal with the masses, a bottleneck formed at the top of the escalator. The pace became annoyingly slow. As I drew nearer, I saw the reason for the pedestrian traffic jam. There were ropes that allowed people to step onto the escalator only one at a time. There was a large sign that read, "CAUTION, when stepping onto the moving stairs, stand in the center of the stair between the two yellow lines! Only one passenger at a time, please."

I was dumbfounded. Here I had been driving and walking through mine fields in Afghanistan for six months, where bombs exploded around me and firefights broke out in my neighborhood—and in London they chose to spend their time and money worrying about how people ride an escalator.

The shock continued as I got home to the States and settled back into my life in Woodland Park. One afternoon Mom and I went to the grocery store to pick up a few items, and I was absolutely overwhelmed with the selections of food. In Afghanistan, we ate beans, rice, and mutton, but in the States there are so many options to choose from. I found myself getting a bit flustered with too many choices, and shopping turned into a stressful event. I could see the looks on the faces of hundreds of skinny, displaced children in Afghanistan who would absolutely freak out if they could see what our average grocery store looks like on the inside. Those kids wake up and go to sleep with hunger pains, and we aren't ashamed to throw out our excess food. I remember thinking as I walked up and down the aisles of food, "This is surely anything but a fair and balanced world we live in."

Settling in took time. My folks were getting ready to move to Afghanistan for a long-term assignment, and I only had a couple weeks with them before their departure, but the time spent was good. The very day my folks flew to Afghanistan, I flew to Las Vegas to collect my personal belongings and say goodbye to friends. After settling all of my affairs in Vegas, I finally gave a long sigh of relief, glad that I was finished traveling for a while. I worked at various jobs for six months as I simply tried to get my feet planted and myself situated in Colorado. Bills were high because of the debt that I had managed to accumulate in Las Vegas. The Colorado Springs economy is not nearly as strong as Las Vegas, where mega-hotel housekeepers start out at $10 an hour, so financial stress mounted, and I once again learned how to place my trust in the Lord. With each passing day, I realized that I was being provided for, and the Lord continued to sustain me in His Love.

I spent a lot of time walking. Never had I noticed the sheer beauty of the Colorado mountains as I did just after returning from Afghanistan. The desert landscape of Afghanistan has its own uniqueness, but the mountains of Colorado are gorgeous.

Spending hours taking walks with the purpose of simply spending quiet time with God, I learned to discern the small and still voice of the Lord in my heart.

I did not know many people in Woodland Park, as many my age were finishing college elsewhere. My folks' home church is called New Covenant Christian Fellowship (NCCF), and I began attending services each Sunday. I vaguely knew the pastor, Chris, because he used to be the youth group leader when I was in high school. My folks reintroduced me to him once I returned from Afghanistan. Chris had given me something just after I graduated high school that had taken the journey of rebellion with me, every step of the way. It was a small Bible, the very Bible that I had taken to Afghanistan. I recall reading the little Bible in Rustaq and noticing that in the front was written, "From Chris Austin. Congratulations! May the Lord go with you in Vegas and where life takes you." I remember thinking how amazing it was that the little Bible had made it through so many moves and times of my life. It was always with me. "How symbolic of the Lord is this!" I thought.

Chris and his wife, Tiffany, helped me get acquainted with some of those who attended NCCF, and before I knew it, I was feeling quite comfortable and a part of the group. It was nice to feel connected. One day Chris and I were at a friend's home, talking about Christianity and faith with a woman. The two of them were deep in a conversation about Christ and the things of redemption when I felt a strong word come to my heart. All three of us were sitting on the floor of the living room. The voice said, "Ask Chris to pray for you." The reply I gave in my heart was, "No, this is their conversation, and I should not interrupt."

It came again with, "Ask Chris to pray for you now." Again, I said in my heart, "No, for it would be rude to butt into their conversation."

"You will ask Chris to pray for you. Do it now," was the word that came again, and this time it was much more authoritative. So I said, "Excuse me. Sorry for butting in, guys." They both looked at me blankly. "Chris, I feel like I'm supposed to ask you to pray for me right now." He looked at me, smiled, and said, "OK."

I sat between Chris and our friend Theresa; they placed their hands on me and Chris started praying. I felt myself begin to shake. A few minutes later, I was laughing. Hysterically. Then, I felt as though I was crying, but no tears came out. I could not stay still. Next, I heard a language in my mind that I did not fully understand, but I knew it had to do with words of praise to the Lord. This went on and on.

When Chris finished, we discussed what it means to receive the empowerment of the Holy Spirit. What a great high! I had never felt such overwhelming pleasure in my life. No sexual escapade, drug-related high, or compliment from another could match this feeling. What love!

I became a full believer in the reality of tongues on that very day in which I began to speak it myself. I did not have to verbally utter a word; the sound of tongues was loud and crisp and beautiful inside my heart. I had not contemplated the theological issues of tongues for many years, and, at the time the gift was given to me, I had not been longing for it. But I was so very thankful for the gift once I had a chance to feel the real power and love that accompanies it!

A few days later, Chris came up to me and said, "I want you to come to Kansas City with me and a small group. We're going to a young adults conference over New Year's, and I think you should go." I told him that I couldn't. I had just started working for one of the elders of the church, and I explained to Chris that I didn't feel I could take time off this soon. Chris persisted over and over. I had no money, so I explained that I could not go on the grounds of money. Still Chris persisted day after day. Finally, he walked up to my boss and me and asked again, "So, are you going to the conference?"

I looked at my boss and asked, "Can I?"

He said, "Sure," so I made a choice at the last minute to go. It turned out to be the most significant decision I had made since choosing to go to Afghanistan. I had no idea what was in Kansas City, but through fate or divine intervention, I found myself on I-70 on the afternoon of December 28, 2002, sitting in the front passenger seat of a van full of teenagers and twentysomethings as Chris drove. I asked him, "So, what is this conference anyway?"

"It's called the One Thing conference, and it is put on by a group called Friends of the Bridegroom," Chris explained. "It is focused on worship and prayer. There will be a lot of music and worship sets in which some notable musicians will be performing. There is also a good amount of teaching and various classes you can go to. It will be a good experience for you."

I had no idea what to expect. Chris had told me that many people planned to fast during the conference, so without much hesitation I decided that I should fast the four-day conference as well. By fasting and really pressing into the Lord during the time in Kansas City, I was sure it would be a spiritually powerful experience. Besides, I had little to no money for food anyway.

We arrived and checked into the conference, and I was shocked to behold the sheer numbers in attendance. There were more than 10,000 young people about my age in a great big conference hall. The stage was huge, and it looked like a million-dollar concert. The experience was powerful for me. I was struck by new revelation about the Lord from the moment the first worship set started, and I can recall going in and out of a state of reality to dreamlike visions and impressions.

At one point, I was standing on my chair and looking over the crowd. There was a sea of heads, and hands were in the air during a worship set. I could see thousands of people, all with one heart to praise the Lord. When I say I went "in and out of a state of reality," it might be better explained in terms of what happened next, as I looked out over the sea of people worshipping. I saw light hit the heads of the overwhelming majority of those worshipping, and I heard a voice in my heart say, "All these people I have picked to be here for this time and purpose. No man or woman is here by accident. I will grow My army in the final hour before My return." Then the light faded, and specific arrows pointed down on the heads of a small percentage of people in the room, and the voice in my heart said, "These few will be radically changed now. Others will grow by the seeds of truth planted during this time." With that, I was back in reality, and the music was loud and clear.

I remember deeply longing to be one of the few whose lives would be radically changed right then. Almost all of the vision or impression-type experiences were deeply personal. Very little seemed to regard anything outside my personal struggles, pain, and growth. One such vision left a lasting mark on my heart.

It was New Year's Eve, and The Call had joined our conference in Kansas City, causing our attendance to grow to some huge number and the spiritual intensity to climax. I could not get over the irony of where I was exactly one year earlier, on New Year's Eve in 2001—the Las Vegas Boulevard when the power of the Lord came over me. I remember pointedly hoping for another experience like that as The Call got underway on December 31, 2002. I had been fasting and was tired and weak, but I felt excited and somehow energized by the endless flow of music and teaching. The Call started at 7:00 a.m. and finished at 1:00 a.m. the morning of January 1, 2003. I loved every minute of it.

The most powerful time of the conference for me was when worship leader Jason Upton performed. As he began to play the keyboards, sing, and speak, I felt a strong spiritual intensity hit the room. It was as though lightning struck the building as Jason Upton continued through his set. I felt overwhelmed with emotion, but I did not know why. He continued to play and sing, and then suddenly I was not in Kansas anymore ...

I opened my eyes and saw myself standing on a balcony in Las Vegas. The sun was setting, and I had a cigarette in my hand. I was looking off into the distance with tears in my eyes. Then I heard myself say, "God, I'm through with You. Go away from me and never come back!" It was at that very moment that I remembered, for the first time since that dreadful day, uttering those words to the Lord. Emotion gripped me as I saw in the spiritual what it did to the Lord, who seemed to be all around me as I stood on that balcony. I watched as the gentle God, cloaked in compassion and love, stepped back from me with tears streaming down His face. It was as though He said to me, "It must be this way, but I will never leave you!"

As I continued to watch this spiritual scene unfold in Vegas, I was aware that I was bitterly weeping in the reality of Kansas City. The scene continued as the Lord showed me how time and time again, I rebelled against Him and His love in defiant acts of disobedience. Soon the scene was too much for me, and I heard myself crying, "Stop, enough, I can't take the reality of my sin!" But the vision continued. I then saw the Lord take the emotional lashings I dished Him through my sin, one by one, until one day I walked back to Him by forcing myself to attend church. He was there with open arms, not caring about hearing me say, "Sorry," or needing some sort of affirming word. He is God, and I saw Him literally crying as I entered the First Baptist Church of the Lakes. I heard Him say, "I will never let you go again. You are mine!"

The scene was too much for me to bear. I forced my eyes open as I begged for forgiveness on the floor. Jason Upton's music became loud again, and I found myself sobbing, realizing for the first time that my Lord is not One who calculates, as much as He is One who feels. Comfort came as God seemed to say, "I've been waiting for eternity for you to come to Me in heart. Thank you."

Who was this perfect and wonderful God? I was beside myself with more questions than answers yet again, but I knew without a doubt that God lives, loves, and is very much active and passionate about my life. God cared about everything from the seemingly insignificant to the dramatically huge. I understood love on a new level because of that spiritual experience.

God cared enough about my rebellious self to listen to me tell

Him to go away. He respected me enough to take a step backward, though it hurt Him to do so. He stood at bay for years as I, time and time again, chose to spit in His face with acts of gross sinful defiance. Through it all, He showed Himself to be full of love and compassion. Finally I found myself in a hole that I had dug with no way out, and in wonderfully childlike fashion, I cried out to Him. He was right there to pull me out, seemingly forgetting or righteously ignoring the last words I had spoken to Him, which were, "Go away and never come back."

The ramifications of this were absolutely mind-boggling to me. God cared enough about me to listen and follow the desires of my deceived heart when I told Him to go away. The Lord's desire for unconditional love was made quite evident to me. He did not will me into existence so I would conditionally follow His decrees and love Him; He willed me into existence so that I might bring my voluntary love to His throne. My voluntary love was more important to the Lord than the pain, mockery, disdain, contempt, and insolence of my rebellion. It was better for Him to be hurt on the account of me denying Him, so that in the future I might come to Him and understand the depth, width, height, and breadth of His love for me and, in turn, bring my love to Him.

What a paradigm shift this was for me. No longer did I see a fat and grumpy old man in the clouds with a name tag on him that read "GOD: Calculus Professor," eating grapes and making big decisions about the orbit of stars and suns. My former and deceived understanding of God was revolutionized as a clearer picture came into focus. I no longer saw the calculus professor, but now I saw the Deity in fire and fierceness, so full of love that wrath boils in His veins because of the injustices of the earth. I saw the One who cares about every blade of grass on earth, and He cares so much more about the thoughts, feelings, pains, rebellions, and emotions of His children!

Another concept that was curiously altered and redefined during that spiritual vision was suffering. I had always seen suffering as an injustice inflicted upon me by some other force or power. I suffered, and so I had cause to be angry and mad about the lack of justice in this earth. "God, where are You, and if You're near, why does suffering exist?" was a very fundamental question during my years of pain and rebellion.

In answering this question, the Lord reminded me that He alone had provided my means to move and settle into Las Vegas. I had prayed for the financial means to move to Vegas, and a Christian family had sent me a check. The first truth was that God is omniscient, which means "all-knowing," and thus knew that I would get into trouble, which would lead to His own feelings of suffering, as well as mine.

Next, He revealed that the Garden of Eden was without fault and devoid of suffering. The second fundamental truth about suffering was that God never wanted man to become defiant and rebellious, but we chose that course and inevitably brought suffering upon ourselves. But suffering, in its essence, was never God's will for us as people.

Thirdly, He revealed that Christ came that He might partake in the fellowship of suffering, so that I might be redeemed from my sinful nature and spend eternity with Him in heaven. Instead of nullifying what we know as suffering, which is the direct root of sin, and effectively canceling His perfect plan of voluntary love, He chose to come here and suffer with us, that we might be bailed out of our damning existence the only way possible!

These three truths about suffering somehow became evident to me when I was flat on my face during the concert in Kansas City.

My prevailing anger toward God about the pain of my past, or the distorted nature of my perspective of pain, kept me from seeing that the sufferings of my life represent the very proof of His perfect plan for me. Had God alleviated suffering as a whole for the human race when we choose to follow our sinful desires, He would have also been alleviating the gift of human choice. Suffering and pain are natural consequences of sin. If we had lost the right to choose whom we might love, follow, and serve, then we would have become like a dog, cat, tree, or insect. Created beings without the ability to choose are no more use to the Lord than inanimate objects like sand, because His desire was never to have an abundance of stuff or matter, but instead to have loving relationships with people like me. The God of hosts became more unveiled during the conference, and the curiosity of a lovesick son was sparked. I would dedicate my life to knowing more.

Abandon Family

Attacking humanism, tearing down denominational barriers, loving the dejected ... Striving for the Abandoned Lifestyle!

The Abandon Family was birthed through a series of visions, later compiled and titled the Abandon Vision whereby the Lord challenged us to discern the times in which we live. Our call is to prepare the way for the return of the King. Though we have various ministry components under the Abandon umbrella, our highest challenge is to strive for the Abandoned Lifestyle as individuals, believing that God is primarily about individual relationship more than corporate movement.

For more information or to request the Abandon Vision be sent to you, please check us out at *www.abandonfamily.com*.

All of the author's rights to any revenues from the sale of this book have been voluntarily signed over to the Abandon Family.